Freediver, surfer and marine biologist by trade, Brinkley Davies has travelled the world for the last decade following her passions for the ocean and wildlife. In 2016, she founded the Balu Blue Foundation, a DGR-endorsed environmental charity that works to protect Australian wildlife and habitats. Then, in 2020, Brinkley launched two new ventures: Bandicoot by Brinkley Jewellery, to help support Balu Blue's conservation projects with sustainable jewellery collections inspired by the sea; and Wildlife Expeditions, which hosts life-changing expeditions to some of the wildest places on earth. Her overall goal is to reconnect people with nature in an incredibly special way.

Well known in the wildlife and marine conservation realms, Brinkley has worked globally on many different campaigns, speaking up for animals all over the world. She works with many brands, including GoPro, Roark Womens and Reef, which sponsor her surfing and freediving. Surfing competitively between the ages of ten and twenty, Brinkley is also a Professional Association of Diving Instructors (PADI) Divemaster and Freedive Instructor. She has a degree in marine biology and more than ten years' experience in the water with marine wildlife. She is also an accomplished photographer and videographer. *Saving Bunji* is her first book.

Saving Bunji

Brinkley Davies

affirm
press

affirm
press

First published by Affirm Press in 2023
Boon Wurrung Country
28 Thistlethwaite Street
South Melbourne VIC 3205
affirmpress.com.au

10 9 8 7 6 5 4 3 2 1

A catalogue record for this
book is available from the
National Library of Australia

ISBN: 9781922863362 (hardback)

Cover design by Luke Causby © Affirm Press
Typeset in Garnett by Emily Thiang
Printed and bound in China by C&C Offset Printing Co., Ltd.

This book is dedicated to Bunji – my best friend, who taught me so much – and to all animals around the world. To the animals that fight so hard to survive against all odds, that fight for their young no matter the consequences, that stare into the face of the evils that humans force on them – and still only express love when rescued.

This book is also dedicated to all the people out there who don't look away, drive past or think someone else will help. To every single person who has ever stopped to help an animal, who has gone out of their way to save a life, who sees the same value in animals as we do in our fellow humans.

Thank you.

Acknowledgement of Country

The following account takes place in various places across Australia.

It takes place in the Eyre Peninsula, South Australia – a place I called home for many years, love dearly and that will always be a part of me. Along with Balu Blue, I acknowledge the traditional owners of the land, the Barngarla people, and pay respects to Elders past and present.

Part of this story also happens in Exmouth and the Nyinggulu Reef in Western Australia. We acknowledge the traditional owners of the land, the Baiyungu, West Thalanyji and Yinikurtura peoples, and pay respects to Elders past and present.

Finally, this story spends significant time in Scamander, Tasmania. We acknowledge the traditional owners of the land, the Pyemmairrener people, and pay respects to Elders past and present.

I hope one day us settlers can exist among wildlife and wild places, and live with a gentle footprint, like the traditional owners did for thousands of years.

When we try to pick out anything by itself, we find it hitched
to everything else in the Universe.

John Muir

When I look into the eyes of an animal, I do not see an animal.
I see a living being. I see a friend. I feel a soul.

Anthony Douglas Williams

Love is found in the most unexpected places;
sometimes it comes to you from the side of the road.

Anastasia Tatarenko, a Bunji fan

CONTENTS

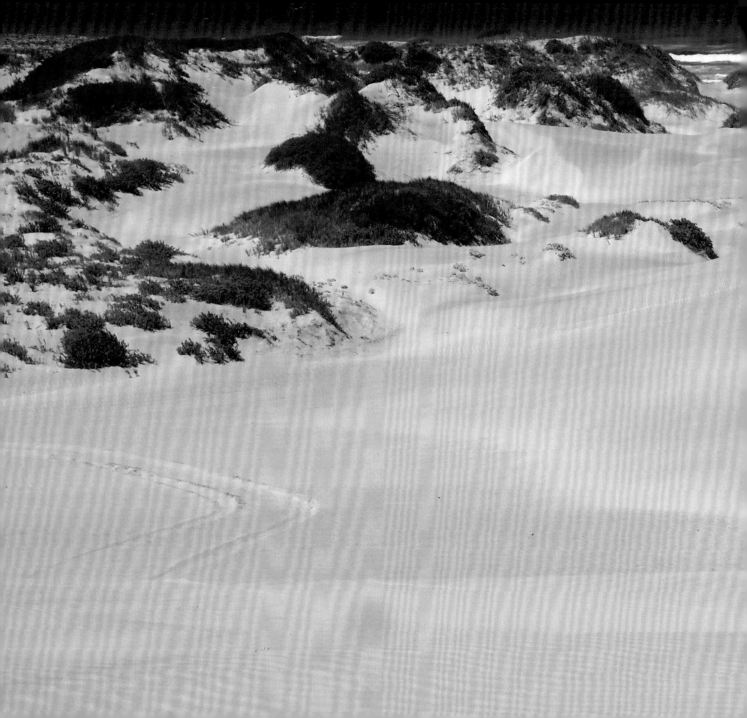

CHAPTER ONE

Growing up in country Australia

Wherever there are wild animals in the world, there is always an opportunity for caring, compassion and kindness.

Paul Oxton

Growing up in country Australia is different. It teaches you a lot of things, and one of them is to have a hard shell. We took long drives down long country roads, often through the night; accidentally hitting wildlife was unfortunately a semiregular experience in these parts. I can remember a few occasions which stood out to me as a passenger, suddenly feeling that sickening thud. Whichever of my parents was driving would quickly brake, then turn to me and say, 'Just stay in the car, okay? Don't look. Put your hands over your ears.'

I'd have all my fingers and toes crossed that whoever was driving would come back and say, 'It was just a pothole,' but it never was. It made me feel sick, often for days at a time. It's a part of my childhood that shaped the rest of my life and my dedication to wildlife.

A lot of my childhood was wonderful, though. It was filled with surfing, my family and friends and (shocker!) animals. My childhood best friend, Hayley, lived about five kilometres away from us by road, but we figured out that sneaking through the backs of people's properties was way quicker and meant our parents didn't have to drop us off. One of the paddocks we used to cross was always full of cows, and one cow in particular had a habit of charging at us. I look back now and laugh, knowing how gentle cows are; one time, as I sprinted to outrun the cow, looking behind me all the while, I ran straight into a head-high fence – an experience known in Australia as being 'clotheslined'. It knocked me out cold. Luckily, I lived to sprint another day.

Hayley's mum Melissa was (and still is) one of my mum's closest friends. When I was a kid, she had a rescue kangaroo called Ruby. Being around that type of rescue scenario definitely influenced my life. Hayley loved animals just like I did; when we weren't full of adrenaline, bouncing on the trampoline, riding bikes or helping our parents maintain our properties, we were spending time with animals.

My family always had pets growing up. There was a cockatiel, Flap, who lived until she was fifteen. Flap was never in a cage; my dad built her a little tree, and she used to fly around our large brick house and sometimes poop on the couch. Dogs were also always a huge part of our family. Chloe, Doroe, Risky, Couch, Mak and Kita were all dogs I had during my childhood.

My parents were animal lovers from way back, and despite maybe not wanting me to bring random animals into the house, they always did what they could. I remember one Mother's Day we were returning from a short break at our holiday house in Marion Bay. My brother and I were desperate to have one last surf before we left, and talked Mum into driving to a popular but secluded surf break. Unfortunately, it wasn't a day for good waves, so we headed home soon after arriving. The area nearby was mainly farming land, quite barren of trees – so when we came across a little lamb on the side of the road in the middle of nowhere, no other sheep anywhere in sight, he was a bit hard to miss. I was very upset by the sight, and made it very clear that we were going to have another passenger in our car for the trip home. Considering that we also had a friend of my brother and our two family dogs in the car, it was a tight squeeze!

My mum fondly remembers the sight of a lamb, two dogs and two children looking out the back seat car window as we drove through the city. We ended up passing the lamb onto a neighbour and family friend who were better suited to care for it. Mum says that day is still one of the most notable Mother's Days she can remember.

My rescue efforts weren't a once-off event, and often happened closer to home. For quite a few years, my dad's main income was foliage; he planted thousands of trees, then harvested the pretty branches to sell to florists as fillers for their flower bunches. Hayley and I used to spend hours in the paddock after school, riding the quad bike, looking for animals and playing hide and seek. It also was pretty common for my brother and I to spend a few hours after school helping Dad pick foliage for pocket money. There were rows upon rows of plants, and often within those rows there were rabbit burrows. On some occasions, I'd find baby rabbits, known as 'kits'. We always tried to put them back into a nearby burrow, but it was difficult to know which burrow they came from, and kits get so terrified and stressed. I'd end up bringing them to the house. Dad made little hutches for them to stay in, and I'd do my best to look after them until they were old enough to be released. Tadpoles were another childhood conservation effort of mine: at certain times of the year, usually towards the end of spring, there would be hundreds of them in our dam. Even though they didn't need any help, I took it upon myself to 'rescue' them. When they got big enough, I'd rerelease them into the dam. I loved watching them grow and change – it probably had a hand in my interest in marine biology, now that I think of it.

One of the other factors might have been my parents' fresh fish and seafood shop, which they owned before the foliage business. They worked super long hours – both at work, then at home – to keep the shop going. Naturally, my family ate a lot of seafood. Everything smelt like fish, but to us, it was just a normal smell. My parents sold many different fish: shellfish, octopus, squid and more. As the years went by, I got so curious about them that I started going to the wholesale fish markets with Dad. I never left feeling good after seeing the animals I loved watching at the beach all laid out, frozen and lifeless. The few times I helped Dad go fishing, I always begged him to throw them back. My family only ever took what they needed, but I just didn't like killing things. The smell of fish became something I grew to dislike, and later on I would stop eating it completely. I understand catching your own food out of necessity, but I still can't understand why people would do it for fun. The people from my parents' generation that I grew up with were wonderful, but there was a distinct difference in how they were taught about animals. Particularly how they categorised animals as 'okay to eat' because they thought certain animals weren't as smart as a cat or a dog, for example. Thankfully, as time goes on, I see more and more people realising just how special and unique all animals are – like my dad, who stopped buying octopus after learning about their incredible intelligence.

My feelings about eating poultry and red meat were the same as my feelings about eating fish. I always questioned what it was, but back then, nobody really wanted to reckon with where it actually came from. After having our sheep, especially our rescue sheep Mambo and our lambs, I connected the dots between our livestock lambs and what we were eating. Looking back, I know now that my parents did an amazing job of feeding us healthy food as kids with the knowledge they had – but I also know that now they would choose to do it differently. At the time, we were told that meat was an essential part of our diet, so it was considered a necessary evil. I think once you have a livestock animal as a pet, it quickly changes your perspective; they're no different to the dogs we consider family, and can love us just as much.

My stubbornness didn't just extend to protecting and caring for animals. A lot of people close to me might say now that I'm driven and dedicated, and I reckon that came from my struggle with taking no for an answer as a kid. I've always gone after the things I want in life or think are right. I can see now how I would have annoyed my parents at times, particularly when it came to surfing.

Surfing has been a huge part of my life since I was young – I first stood up on a surfboard when I was about four years old, maybe younger! When I was a kid, it was my favourite thing on earth to do. Any chance my older brother, Jedd, and I had, we would be in the water. We often used to go to our holiday house on the Yorke Peninsula, where I learnt to surf waves that scared the life out of me with Jedd, Dad and a few friends of friends. I was, more often than not, the only girl in the line-up. The rest were boys ranging from ten all the way up to my dad's age, and even older. It wasn't as intimidating as it sounds; if I felt scared, I had the support of way more experienced and skilled surfers. They told me when to sit deeper and paddle harder, or how to tell if a set was coming. As I learnt to surf, I was surrounded by wildlife of all kinds; the closeness to sea creatures was one of my favourite things about surfing.

It was perfect, and by the time I was nine, I was 100 per cent set on being a professional surfer and began competing. While there were a bunch of good surfers in South Australia, only a few girls competed and hardly any were my age. I often went up against the boys, and sometimes I'd even wind up in the same heat as Jedd, which didn't end well for the car trip home. It taught me from a young age not to feel threatened by men in general, something that's done wonders for my career and self-confidence. Competing was empowering, and besides, I loved surfing – so in competitions with a time limit and varying conditions, I felt it really pushed my surfing the most. During a competition, I had to go out and try to catch my two best waves, even if it was scary or out of my comfort zone; I had to force myself through my fears and doubts and focus on doing my best. Looking back, it was the largest part of my childhood and taught me so much about how to approach success and failure.

Growing up, there was one competition I cared about the most: the Yorkes Classic, which was always held at one of the heavier waves on the Yorke Peninsula. This wave was always on my backhand, and had both a section for turns and a barrel. It broke over a shallow reef, and only had a single tiny reef passage you could pass through – and even then, you had to time going in and out between sets. The only category for women in the Yorkes Classic then was Open Women. The first year I decided to enter, I was twelve. I went up against women more than double my age.

But I loved a challenge, and to be riding the biggest and most powerful wave at Chinamans, in a heat for that competition, was the most fun and rewarding competition I can remember doing. After getting comfortable out there and knowing the

wave better, I went on to win the Open Women event for four to five years in a row. My parents also used to take us to the Rusty Gromfest competition in Lennox Head. Rusty Gromfest was held in smaller, junkier waves, but we were up against other teenagers who were fiercely competitive and really good surfers, with all kinds of tactics. That world was new to me; it taught me how to surf in crowds and read line-ups from a young age. Unfortunately, that part of competitive surfing was what would ultimately steer me away from the competition scene.

I surfed all the way through my teenage years, but the reality of competing hit hard. The world of the qualifying series was challenging and expensive; most competitors my age had financial support from sponsors, or their parents funded their way. My parents were doing their best to support me, and I even had a sponsor, which was amazing – but the sponsor only saw me as a competitor and not a person, which was dehumanising. There was so much pressure to perform from both outside and within, and the actual competitions weren't particularly thrilling. I was travelling to surf crappy 2-foot waves with aggressive girls from overseas who didn't even want to talk to me. Not to mention, the wildlife was almost always absent.

As I got to the end of school, I did the big pregraduation soul search. Competitions were ruining the joy of surfing for me, and my passion for the lifestyle was fading. I found myself thinking about whether it was worth it.

Is this what I want to do? Does this make me happy? I couldn't stop thinking about how, at home, I had big, perfect waves, dolphins and a clean ocean. That was where I loved to surf most, so I decided I would make it happen professionally.

I started putting effort back into surfing where and how I loved to, hoping that some of my sponsors would support my freesurfing ventures. I also started making films with videographers with a focus on conservation. This was a huge transitional period away from surfing as a competitive sport to surfing as a vessel for telling stories the ocean had taught me. This hard work would later result in a few major surfing sponsors supporting me as a whole package, not just as a girl in a rashie trying to make heats.

Surfing wasn't the only thing I carried a torch for through my teenage years; I was still keeping an eye out for animals in need. It was as a teenager that I took up my first ever volunteering role with animals. I signed up as a TLC volunteer at my local RSPCA, which basically meant I kept dogs and cats company by hanging out with them at the shelter. I went at least once a week. Some days I'd hang out with dogs who had anxiety or had come from scary living situations; I'd sit in their kennel with them and do my homework, or read to them and myself. Other days, I'd go in the kitten pens, and just let them crawl over me and play with them. My role was to help them learn to trust humans again. It was so rewarding and, at the same time, heartbreaking. I wanted to take them all home, and it made me so passionate about adopting animals as well as promoting the need to know where your pets have come from.

My time at the RSPCA was an amazing entry into animal care, and I started looking for volunteer work with marine wildlife. In South Australia, it was quite hard to come by, but luckily one organisation was doing some great work – the Australian

Marine Wildlife Research and Rescue Organisation (AMWRRO).
I ended up meeting Aaron, the founder, and he taught me
a lot about animals in care. My time at AMWRRO consisted
of preparing food for the animals, cleaning up pens and
administering medicine. It wasn't glamorous; I regularly
blended up frozen fish smoothies for the seabirds! We also
cared for a variety of seals. One, a young Australian fur seal
pup called Emma, was emaciated and needed to be brought
back to good health. I really connected with Emma. She was
the most beautiful seal I had ever seen. I'd clean out her pen
and sometimes just sit with her. It was a hard balance to
strike. She was to be rereleased into the wild, so we didn't want
her to become too familiar with humans – but seals and sea
lions are curious and very expressive animals, so she soon had
a special place in my heart.

One memorable rescue was a juvenile elephant seal, who
had rocked up on one of South Australia's southern beaches
looking unwell. It isn't uncommon for Antarctic species to
wind up in Southern Australian waters, especially after big
storms. This elephant seal had a huge laceration thanks to a
circular piece of commercial-grade plastic that had wrapped
tightly around her neck. Seals and sea lions are particularly
susceptible to this fate, as they have no way of removing
the plastic themselves – we are their best bet for help. This
seal's particular injuries were close to being fatal. Thankfully
we watched her heal over time, and eventually she was
rereleased.

My time at AMWRRO was so rewarding and memorable.
I learnt a huge amount, and it seeded the idea that we
needed more resources to help animals in need. Between
my volunteering and the strong respect and love for marine

wildlife that surfing had instilled in me, I decided I wanted to learn as much as I could by studying marine biology. However, it wasn't what I thought it was going to be. The first year of studying to be a marine biologist was a bit of an anticlimax. It involved a lot of mandatory basic biology and chemistry, and learning about immunology and diseases. I always got my work done, though – unless the surf that day was good. It was hard to sit through a chemistry lecture knowing the waves were four feet and glassy.

My degree also made it clear to me that there were still systemic issues around how we approached wildlife research. I found animal testing barbaric and unnecessary. In some lab classes, we were asked to dissect fish or crabs – killed purely for that purpose – to learn about their anatomy ... even though we could find detailed anatomical illustrations of almost all animals online. I opted out, choosing to learn from these illustrations instead.

These kinds of ethical issues carried into other areas too. At one point during my immunology course, we were shown an underground laboratory with a variety of animals being subjected to tests. Scientists would infect an animal with a disease or virus to study the level of suffering the animal endured and how it might be cured. I knew about this practice, of course, but it made me physically ill to see it in person. I was disgusted and immediately left. I'm passionately against animal testing. Some people argue animal testing is necessary to develop human vaccines and so on, but humans are smart enough to grow entire organs from tiny cells – surely we can come up with an option that doesn't involve torturing animals?

Though my time at university was challenging, it was also wonderful. I made some great friends there, learnt so much and also did my first certified freedive course around this point. Freediving wasn't such a big thing back then – in fact, barely anyone was doing it. I had done a fair bit of heavy water training at some of the surf camps I went to a few years beforehand, but I had never freedived before; it was entirely new to me, and a skill that would become a huge part of my professional life.

I also became a certified scuba diver; I had always had an interest in getting my certification, especially as I knew it would lead to getting more work.

I moved to Port Lincoln after I received a job offer to work on a marine tourism boat that took guests cage diving with great whites off the Neptune Islands. It was a multifaceted role: I would be an in-water guide, deckhand and marine biologist – it was the best news and greatest professional opportunity I could have asked for, and also meant I could educate customers and passengers about sea lions and sharks.

Growing up as a surfer in South Australia, I had a huge respect for sharks. There really is no feeling like seeing a shadow the size of a car pass under your surfboard. It's almost an out-of-body experience. You feel so, so small. The surfing community in South Australia saw many near-misses and a few big losses of people close to home which instilled a fear of being attacked.We all lived remote, and great white attacks were almost always fatal. Unfortunately, this meant some people believed in trying to kill them off. This fear and aggression towards sharks is something I am determined to dispel where possible, and I like to think that during my time working as a guide, I've done a lot for the cause.

Working on that boat was a dream. Some of the sea lions had gotten to know me and other staff members since we were in the water with them every day. We would hook the boat out to a mooring offshore and swim around in the crystal-clear water. Any sea lion that was awake would see it as an opportunity to play. They would dive past me like a torpedo, twisting, turning, jumping out of the water, always with one eye on me. They reminded me of labradors, and I learnt how they liked to mess around. I'd lie on the bottom, hiding in the seaweed, and let them sneak up on me. They'd swoop around my head, sometimes going behind me and giving me a little tap with their front flippers. It was like another world. Nothing else mattered at that point; this is where I was meant to be. I wanted everyone to know how special these animals were, how incredible they were. I had seen seals and sea lions growing up in the surf and helped care for them during my time at AMWRRO – but being in the water with them was something else entirely.

During this time, I got my Open Water, the first dive ticket you can get. After that, I went on to gain my Advanced Open Water and my Rescue Diver certifications, which I did when I was in Hawai'i in 2015. Me and my partner at the time, Ty, had decided to go to Hawai'i for as long as we could, which was three months; we wanted to surf and dive all day every day. This meant I had an opportunity to not only do my diving certifications, but also to volunteer in some toothed whale research projects on the Big Island.

We spent our time in Hawai'i living on the north shore, right in front of Sunset Beach. We made some great friends, ate a lot of fruit and endlessly surfed and freedived. I actually paddled into some of the biggest waves I had ever seen –

sadly, this was cut short when I dislocated my shoulder at a shore break, resulting in having to wear a sling for six weeks and not a whole lot of swimming! We eventually had to leave Hawai'i to ensure we didn't overstay our visa, so we decided to fly straight to Fiji. I had been chatting to the team at Beqa Adventure Divers there, tossing around the idea of doing some dives with them and the bull sharks. Mike, the owner, had a really inspirational story: upon learning about the killing of sharks for income in that area for many years, he started a dive centre. The diving and ecotourism led to the sharks being actively protected, while offering locals a job in ecotourism instead of unsustainable fishing. I thought it was incredible.

We did many dives in Beqa, but diving with a hundred bull sharks never got old and was unlike anything I had ever experienced. It was done in a way that meant you didn't feel intimidated or threatened. We would all be on scuba in a line, with one of the divemasters in the middle and some behind us, to make sure no bull sharks came too close from behind, where we couldn't see them. The sharks didn't like the bubbles that came from our regulators as we breathed out, acting as a natural buffer, but they weren't really interested in us at all. The sharks there are fed, which made sense: they had been fed for decades by fishermen to ensure the size of the fish population stayed as large as possible. Now they were being fed in a controlled way, with crates of tuna and the like, and being attracted to that area meant they were now in a protected marine reserve, safe from harm. I'd never been a fan of shark feeding before that, but seeing the benefits it had to the local population was astounding.

The shark feeders respected the sharks and didn't try to mess with them. They would read the way the sharks approached, and never let things get out of hand. It's an experience I'd recommend to everyone.

After we spent time in Beqa, Ty returned to Australia for work, and I flew back to Hawai'i for four weeks as a research assistant on the toothed whale boat. I was so excited to be working in a field I was passionate about, but mostly very keen to see some of the whale species there in real life. It was a challenging few weeks: big days, long hours, and lots of what I'd call 'tall poppy syndrome' between the head researcher and us volunteers. We were there out of passion, stoked for marine life, whereas it seemed to me that the head researcher was there purely for data and had lost any passion for animals in their own right. That was another trip where I learned that not all marine biologists love animals, and nor would they always see eye to eye with me. We used heavy-duty equipment for tagging and biopsy samples, which, although it has its place in research, is absolutely invasive and shouldn't be in the hands of people who don't respect animals. Tagging the whales in this way made me feel super uncomfortable. I'd been involved in tagging before, but shooting an animal point blank from only a few metres away with a high-powered weapon (which is how you attach a tag!) seemed cruel and inefficient. I kept thinking, *Who is this benefitting, really? The animals, or someone trying to tick off a PhD?* There's absolutely a difference between doing things right and doing things like a cowboy scientist; the former was what I strived for. If only there was a way I could help change things – and little did I know, I was about to get the chance to do so. Unfortunately, it would begin with a terrible, awful accident.

CHAPTER TWO

An unexpected loss

I do have reasons for hope: our clever brains, the resilience of nature, the indomitable human spirit, and above all, the commitment of young people when they are empowered to take action.

Jane Goodall

After we returned to Port Lincoln, our home was a bit quiet. With the sea lions' puppy-like behaviour on my mind, I quickly realised what was missing: a dog. I was used to being around dogs after growing up with them, and I had only held off getting one of my own because I wasn't sure what the future held. After having the realisation that living on the coast would be a great environment for a dog, I had a chat with my parents, who promised they could care for a dog if something happened to me or I had to be away for work. We decided to go to the Port Lincoln RSPCA and have a look. It was a tiny shelter, but with the number of local farms and working dogs, litters of puppies were often dumped there in addition to the adult dogs who had been mistreated and needed loving homes.

When we arrived, there had been a box of border collie–mix puppies left out the front only the day before. I was baffled – how could anyone leave a bunch of baby animals on a doorstep? – and overjoyed. It was perfect timing. I couldn't go home without adopting one, and immediately fell in love with a little boy in the litter. He seemed fluffier than the others, with a soft black coat and a white patch on his chest, and was really gentle-natured. Luckily, he was still up for adoption, so we paid the fee and took him home. I'll never forget driving along the front street of Port Lincoln with him on my lap, how he took his first sniffs of fresh ocean air as he stared out the window. A new life was ahead of him, and I'd never been more excited. After the first week, between his caring, gentle nature and cuddle-bear looks, we named him Balu – like the bear from *The Jungle Book* – but with our own little twist.

The months that followed were full of adventure, especially when my hours working on the boat were cut back to a few days a week. I really started getting into photography and flying my drone, as well as focusing once more on my surfing. Balu came on these adventures with us, and learnt to stay on the cliff and lie near my things. At our regular surf breaks, the beaches were vast, empty – a dog's dream playground. Balu came to love the car and the long drives, even the boat. Once I went out to surf at an island near Elliston and he went on the boat with me, watching everything pass by as we cruised along. Once I had dropped anchor, I jumped out onto my board to paddle out to the wave. On a whim, I said 'hup' to him, to see if he would climb onto my back to come for a paddle – and he did! He came for a little ride around on my shoulders before I popped him back into the boat while I went for a surf. Balu and I did everything together; he was like my shadow.

After the summer in Port Lincoln that year, I was offered an opportunity to help out on a whale shark research boat for the winter season in Exmouth, Western Australia. We would be studying whale shark migratory patterns and general health. I'd been working hard for an opportunity like this: I had my Coxswain license (a commercial skipper's ticket, which research boats require), experience in shark research and, of course, all my dive certifications. I had been up to Exmouth as a teenager to do work experience, and I had fallen in love with the place. The local beaches and ocean were beautiful; I knew I could easily live there, and it was an opportunity too good to pass up. As it was a volunteer role, accommodation was provided as well. It was just a matter of packing my bag and going.

Ty was working as an abalone diver, and he wasn't able to take the time off and come up for the season with me. Because I was going to be out on the boat all day every day up there, I decided it was best for Balu to stay in Port Lincoln with Ty. Although I was sad to leave them for a few months, I knew that this role could lead to some great work, and if all went well, maybe we could even move there.

When autumn came around, I held Balu tighter than ever before jumping on a plane and heading up to the North-West. I was heartbroken, but I was also so excited to be heading somewhere that really called to me. I couldn't wait to see where this trip led me – but then, about four weeks in, I received the phone call that changed everything.

I had just gotten home from a day on the boat when Ty called me. Calls from Ty were a daily thing; I particularly loved Facetiming Balu. But when I picked up the phone, I could barely understand him. His voice kept breaking as he tried to get words out between tears.

'What happened?' I asked, with the worst sinking feeling in my chest, creeping slowly up to my throat. My hands were shaking. Ty never cried, and we had been through some hard times together.

After a moment, he was finally able to get the words out: 'Balu is dead.'

I'll never forget that moment. It was like someone ran me over and punched me in the stomach. I couldn't breathe. As we both struggled to calm down, Ty managed to explain what had happened. They had been heading down the long country road that leads to the beach we always went to. Ty had to stop to go to the toilet. He had done it many times before along this road. Balu got out too and went to the toilet in the bushes on the side of the road, which bordered a farm fence. A few hours later, not long after Ty got back from the beach, Balu started acting weird. He was disoriented, vomiting, and whimpering uncontrollably – clearly in a huge amount of pain. Ty rushed him to the vet, who told him that Balu had eaten a 1080 bait and wouldn't survive. Balu's life ended right there at the vet, just like that.

Farmers, agricultural companies and - most disturbingly - the National Parks and Wildlife and Department of Environment use highly toxic baits to cruelly control displaced introduced species such as foxes, and rabbits, but most disturbingly, dingoes, our only native canid, which are referred to as 'wild dogs' to justify targeting them. I had heard about these baits, but I hadn't really known about their effects. When a susceptible animal swallows them, they suffer extreme, prolonged pain before finally dying; in dogs, initial symptoms include vomiting, anxiety and shaking. From there, it turns into frenzied behaviour with running and screaming fits, and seizures. Though 1080 baits are supposedly strategically laid, there's no real guarantee that they won't be carried elsewhere by birds or eaten by animals that aren't the target – like poor Balu.

Balu's death didn't seem real to me. I was in shock for a few hours, which became a few days. I wasn't able to go to work, or be around other people. My heart had shattered into a million pieces, and I didn't know what to do about it. I was heartbroken, angry, lost. I decided to go home to Port Lincoln, to process all of this, and be with Ty.

Back in Port Lincoln, life had a stark emptiness. We decided to get away for a bit, so we packed up our car and headed west for a few weeks – to surf, camp and do the things we loved to feel happy again without our dog. We hit the road early the next day, stopping in at a few places and surfing a wave we surfed a lot, called 'Blacks', in Elliston. Balu had been a local at this car park; he watched us from the cliff regularly when we surfed, and hung out with the other surfers' dogs. It was our first time there without him. After going for a surf and heading into town to grab a few things from the supermarket, we decided to head up to the cliff to watch the sunset as a way of remembering him.

The road we took back to the cliff was renowned for kangaroos, especially at dusk and dawn, and lined with shrubs on either side that made it difficult to see any incoming animals. We were always on alert driving it, but at this time of the day, the sun's glare was lethal, coming in like fire. Ty slowed right down to about forty kilometres per hour, but no matter how hard we were focusing, it was incredibly hard to see any peripheral movement.

And then, all of a sudden, we heard the bang.

CHAPTER THREE

Saving Bunji

Dare to reach into the darkness, to pull someone into the light.

Norman B. Rice

It was the type of bang no one ever wants to hear in the car, especially on a country road, at dusk in a large 'Troopy' Landcruiser. It was small enough that it wasn't crystal clear whether we had hit a roo or just popped a tyre. Ty stopped the car and got out.

I was whispering to myself, 'Please don't be a roo, please don't be a roo,' when I heard Ty say 'shit'. My heart sank. So many scenarios were playing in my head as I got out of the passenger side to go investigate. Was the roo going to be only partially injured, or were we going to have to put her down? Was it a lone male, or a mum with a joey? Some scenarios were far worse than others.

As I rounded the back of the car, Ty was already handing me a tiny little baby. It was the smallest joey I had ever seen, smooth and pink and furless. A living jellybean. It fit into the palm of my hand and felt so unbelievably light. I quickly checked it for wounds, being as thorough but gentle as I could. It had a minor graze on its backside, but aside from that, seemed perfectly fine – for now. Joeys are very vulnerable to stress, and can easily fall victim to a condition known as myopathy. Myopathy happens when the animal is under extreme stress, caused by circumstances such as cold temperatures or losing its mother. It causes a disintegration of the muscle fibres, which can eventually lead to fatal paralysis.

I knew all of the warning signs of myopathy and stress; ongoing vocalisations and body trembles were the most obvious, symptoms the joey was certainly displaying. Of course, it had just been thrown out of a warm home onto a cold bitumen road. I immediately put it down my top, where, underneath my three layers of clothes and directly against my skin, it would be safe from the cold. It would also be the closest way to mimic the environment it would have been in – Mum's pouch. As soon as I put it down there, it immediately settled and relaxed into my chest. I was relieved, and frankly amazed it had survived. If a joey is really, really tiny, its mouth is usually still fused to a teat inside the mother kangaroo's pouch; removing it before it unfuses naturally is typically fatal. At the same time, I also had a sinking feeling in my stomach. Ty was still gone. Where was the mum?

After living with me, Ty was well acquainted with wildlife rescue, and as a caring person who regularly drove in rural areas, he was used to checking on animals. If he hadn't come back to the car to check on me and the joey, it wasn't good. I called out to him and asked what was happening, and he said, 'Don't come over here.' That told me it was one of two options: the mum had already passed away, or she was struggling and needed someone to end her suffering.

The roos I saw regularly and around here were Euro kangaroos, which are a smaller, fluffier species also known as 'wallaroos'. Part of me thought maybe it was a relatively little one that had passed quickly on impact – the best-case scenario. The larger species, such as red kangaroos and grey kangaroos, or larger wallaroos, will often survive against crazy odds and incur fatal injuries such as spinal or head injuries and broken hind limbs. When this happens, someone needs to put them down – and in rural Australia, where there are hardly any wildlife vets to come out and help, that someone is you. Ideally, in these situations you'd have access to a gun and be able to quickly end their suffering, but we didn't have one. We'd have to bludgeon it to death. The idea made me want to throw up, but it was better than leaving it to slowly die for days as ants and crows devoured it alive.

I'd been in the car before when someone had to euthanise wildlife like that, usually because another person had hit the animal and just kept driving. Millions of native animals are hit each year by motor vehicles on Australian roads, and many people don't stop. I can understand it – they don't want to think about what has happened, so they simply push it to the back of their mind and keep driving – but it's an awful thing to do. If you stop, at worst you'll have to end the animal's suffering – but leaving it there means the animal may suffer in agony for days. I have pulled hundreds of dead animals off the road, checked roo pouches to find the joey dead, and had animals pass away in my arms. Every single one was awful, but at least I knew I had tried.

With all this racing through my mind, I prepared myself for the worst as Ty came back to the car. The mother kangaroo had quickly passed, he told me. I was heartbroken but relieved that she hadn't suffered, that we didn't have to go through what I had been through before. I was also glad that it was our car that hit her and not someone before or after us – someone who might have kept driving.

I felt the joey shift against my chest. I would do everything I could to keep it alive in the months to follow.

Warmth, quiet, and an audible heartbeat. These three things help stabilise a baby joey immediately. Then comes nutrients, specialised care, a lot of patience and dedication. Although I knew what was needed, I was eager to ensure I was doing everything right. I started reaching out to all my wildlife carer contacts to double-check the next steps. I was 100 per cent in to give this baby a fighting chance.

At this point, we were back in Elliston. It was dark, we were living out of our Troopy, and now I had an approximately four-week-old kangaroo joey down my top. It was a lot to take in. I knew now that the joey was a girl. She didn't have testes, and even when they are tiny, female joeys still have a pouch. It looks like a little hole or skin flap on their belly – and she had one. I was reluctant to name her, because survival rates of pinkys – young joeys that haven't yet grown fur – is so low. I didn't want to get attached until we had gotten past the first forty-eight hours. This period is crucial.

First on the list was to get some formula: joeys at this size suckle every two to three hours, maybe more. It would also be comforting for her to have a bottle with a teat, just like her mum's pouch would have had. The formula I was after is known as Wombaroo Milk Replacer 0.4. There are very specific guides to which formula a joey needs, depending on how far along they are. My little girl was furless, but her skin was darkening, her eyes had just opened and her little ears weren't stuck to her head. She met the criteria perfectly for 0.4 formula. This can usually be found at vet clinics, but of course, we were nowhere near one. I didn't have any formula in the rescue pack we kept in the car, either – lesson learnt.

We were in luck, though. After a few phone calls, some friends who lived on a property near Elliston had the correct formula as they had raised quite a few joeys. We headed there straight away, picked up the formula, a bottle and new rubber teat that was correct for her size/weight, and then made our way to a spot where we could set up for the night.

Next on the list was setting up the perfect environment for her. One of the most difficult things about caring for a joey this small is that they need help regulating their body temperature. They can easily get too cold, or too hot. There are specially made heat mats available for this very purpose, but they weren't exactly readily available at midnight in the middle of the Eyre Peninsula. Luckily, my body temperature was exactly what she needed, so the ideal place was still on my chest. I used a pillowcase as a mini pouch, placing it down my top and on my skin, and then pulling the open top of the pillow case up through the neck of my jacket. She was so happy down there, and the opening meant she was getting much-needed fresh air (although joeys have an incredible tolerance for carbon dioxide!). With that set up, we boiled some water on our cooker and took it off the heat to let it cool. You can test for the right temperature the same way you would test it for a human baby: putting a tiny bit of the water on your wrist. I used a scalpel to poke a tiny little hole in the rubber teat and once the water was cool enough, I mixed in the correct amount of formula. It's important to ensure that the milk isn't too hot or cold, as this can further stress out the joey.

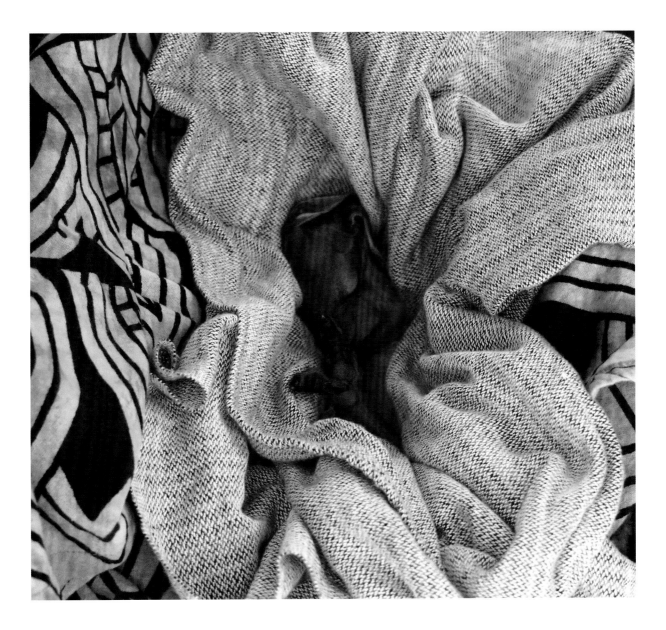

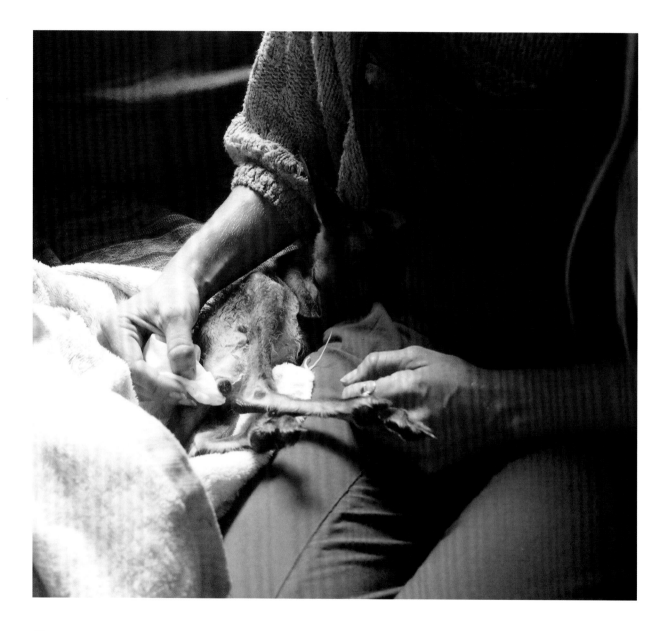

Once everything was finally ready, I slowly and so, so gently moved the little pillowcase pouch inside my beanie. That way, I could bring her head out enough to feed her and she would still be warm. As she was tiny, her mouth was also tiny, and very much closed. One of the biggest challenges we faced was getting her to open up so we could gently slide the teat into her mouth. We let a tiny bit of formula come up on the teat first, and just rubbed it gently on her lips, hoping she might taste it and open her mouth enough to get the teat in. After a little while, it worked – she was sucking! – but it wasn't enough for milk to come out of the bottle. I had to squeeze the bottle a teeny bit. It took her about half an hour to drink 5 to 10 millilitres, and all I could think was *progress*. It was a miracle. I thought, *is this what it's like for mums when their babies finally latch on while breastfeeding?* It gave me a whole new appreciation for how new mothers must feel. The relief, the joy, the affection. I was in love.

Given her age and weight, I was guessing she was going to need about fix to six feeds a day, once every three hours or so. I was thinking mostly about my sleep, or the forthcoming lack thereof. It was okay, though. I'd gone into full mother mode and was ready for it – among other things, such as toileting.

Most people don't know that joeys can't go to the toilet by themselves. In the wild, the mother kangaroo will lick them clean inside the pouch until they are old enough to be outside and regularly eating solids. This licking is how the joey knows to go to the toilet. Wildlife carers have to simulate this for rescues by 'toileting' them, which involves using a warm, wet cloth to stimulate around the joey's cloaca.

Toileting is a vital way of knowing how the joey's health is; given that our tiny little rescue had just been through a huge ordeal, and was likely dehydrated, I was surprised and relieved that as I toileted her, she did a little wee and poo. Just like that, we had established a routine, and she was settled enough for us to start her recovery process.

I cleaned her and popped her back down my jumper in the pillowcase, and we got into our Troopy bed. I sleep on my back and don't move at all during the night, so I wasn't worried about squishing her at all. As I lay down, I felt her snuggle in even tighter to me. We had made it through the first few hours, and I felt good about it. By the time I closed my eyes it was about 2am. I set my alarm for four hours' time, and off to sleep I went.

I woke up before my alarm. I feel like that always happens when you have an important job to do, and motherhood is at the top of the important jobs list. Our little rescue joey was still sound asleep on me, not surprising at all given her ordeal the day before. I went back to sleep for another hour or so before starting the day and, most importantly, starting our caring routine.

This time around it was much easier to get her to grab onto the teat. Even though she was only drinking a tiny amount at her age, it was a relief each time. I figured out that if I put some milk on my pinky finger then rubbed it on her mouth, she would try to latch onto my finger, creating a gap I could gently slide the bottle teat into. Pinkys' mouths are very delicate, so you always have to be extra careful to avoid damaging their still-developing palate.

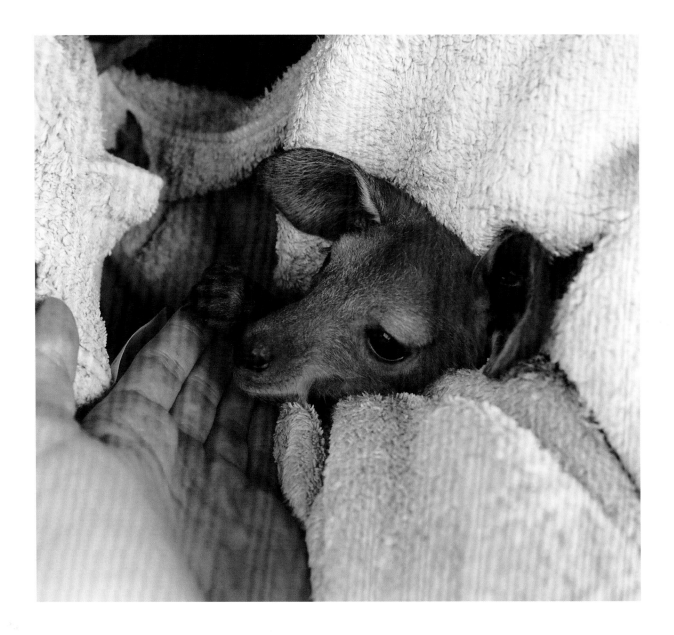

We also had a hot water bottle to act as a secondary source of warmth for her if I needed to put her down, and we made a secure little pouch for her to hang out in over the car headrest, where we could add the hot water bottle along with padding.

After the first forty-eight hours passed, we thought it best we head back to Port Lincoln to settle in and set up our little room for my new charge. The joey had survived through the few crucial days, and I already adored her. I still missed Balu terribly, of course, but caring for this joey had given me something to focus on. Earlier in the year I had been researching Indigenous names for future pets. 'Bunji' had been one of my favourites, coming from Warlpiri and other languages of the traditional owners of the Northern Territory and Northern Queensland. It means 'a close friend and kinsman' – and that's exactly how I felt about the little joey I was literally carrying around on my heart. It was the perfect name for her.

CHAPTER FOUR

Making a home joey-friendly

Cherish the natural world because you are a part of it,
and you depend on it.

Sir David Attenborough

Upon arriving home, we created a day hang-out spot for Bunji, and really got our routine solid with feeding and toileting. She was now stable, and although she seemed totally fine, I thought it was best to get an official all-clear from a local vet. However, the vet told us that Bunji was a red kangaroo, which she definitely wasn't. Bunji was absolutely a Euro, a very different animal to a red kangaroo. The distinction affects feeding regimes, treatment and more. It seemed that between myself and the other wildlife carer guiding me, we knew a whole lot more than the vet, which was concerning, but not uncommon. Unfortunately, not by any fault of their own, many standard vets are not trained or experienced in handling and caring for wildlife and understanding their particular needs. With this in mind, we told the vet she was stable, feeding and toileting well, and just asked that he do an X-ray to confirm she didn't have any hidden injuries. We got the all-clear from the X-ray, which was great news, and he sent us home. It was a bit frustrating that the vet wasn't more helpful, but I knew the wildlife carers I was in touch with at the time were the best people to lean upon. They had decades of experience, and knew what was needed and what to do in certain situations. Between their knowledge and my own training and experience, I was confident Bunji was safe in my hands.

For the first few weeks, it was all about getting Bunji into a consistent schedule. The first two weeks were rough; we were feeding and toileting her every three hours. I don't think I really knew what sleep deprivation was until this. Ty and I took turns, which made things a bit more bearable, but I had a whole new level of respect for people who regularly cared for pinkys. When Bunji started really guzzling milk from the bottle, though, she could drink more, meaning the feeds could be more spaced apart. We started only getting up once in the night for a feed and toilet around 3am. Then we moved to feeding her three to four times a day: morning, midday, late afternoon and then again around 9 or 10pm. She started sleeping the whole way through the night – thank god!

During this, I was working only two to three days a week on the boat, and two days in a clothes store, which was for the most part pretty quiet. In the store, Bunji would hang out the back in her little makeshift pouch or I'd carry her in my top; on my breaks, I would feed and toilet her, and she slept the rest of the time. The store I worked in was owned by a friend of mine, who loved animals as much as I did. She didn't mind my little passenger at all!

Back home, we bought one of those specialised heat mats online. This was perfect as it meant we could leave it on all day, and never worry about the temperature being too hot or cold. Despite this, at night Bunji slept in bed with us. If we tried to leave her in her pouch at night, she would make the little chirps joeys make when they are unhappy. Even if stress wasn't dangerous for joeys, it's a sound you can't ignore. Bunji would even stay in bed for a while after we got up; with the blanket over her, she was happy as ever, safe and warm.

It was amazing to watch Bunji grow. At first, her skin darkened and then developed a fine layer of fur when she was around three months old. At this stage, joeys will start to get a little curious and begin to poke their heads out of the pouch to see what's going on outside, as well as starting to experiment with nibbling on things like grasses and shrubs. Depending on their species, joeys often don't actually venture out of the pouch until they are five or six months old; mother kangaroos have very strong muscles that control the opening of the pouch, keeping the joey in. When the joey is old enough, the mother relaxes these muscles and lets the joey tumble out, allowing it to return to the pouch as needed.

When Bunji started to stick her head out of her 'pouch' (my jumper), I had a bit of a scout around online to see if there were any alternatives that would be more comfortable for her and less likely to stretch out my clothes. I ended up ordering a super-special handmade bag. It had little mesh windows for her to see out of, plus I could wear it like a backpack and go for walks or even gentle jogs with her inside. (Kangaroo mums obviously don't hesitate to hop around with their joeys in their safe little pouch, after all.) When the bag arrived, I created a very squishy, comfortable little environment inside for Bunji, and taking her with me as I went about my day became a regular activity. We went for walks, headed down to the beach, moseyed around the backyard, hung up the washing, even made dinner together. She loved the movement, sometimes sleeping for hours, and as she grew and peeked out more and more as I walked around, she became familiar with common sounds and smells. Her growing love for gentle motion extended to trips in the car, which, thanks to her unique start in life, she was already comfortable with.

We would hang her new bag off the headrest to simulate hanging off me. She still came with me to work at the shop, and my friend was happy to let me carry her in the bag. Bunji certainly surprised a few customers, who were always delighted by the unexpected appearance – who could blame them?

As Bunji started to get more and more curious, she started nibbling on things. Kangaroos are grazing herbivores, and munch mainly on grasses. I introduced her to she-oak, and she never looked back. Bunji's species is renowned for living on coastal cliffsides and making homes out of native shrubs, so this was no surprise. When she was around five months old, she started really eating solids in an addition to her three to four bottles a day. We would hang a small branch of she-oak over her pouch and she would poke her head out, grab it with her tiny paws and munch happily away before falling back asleep in her pouch.

With the introduction of some solids into her diet came changes to her milk formula and toileting routines. We began slowly introducing a new, more suitable formula to make sure there were no upset tummies. Joeys are very sensitive to changes in their day-to-day life, and any upset is always clear in their poo. After introducing solids into her diet, Bunji was beginning to pass more clearly formed pellets, which were an amazing sign of healthy growth. Unfortunately, the slightest change could cause diarrhea: a door slamming from the wind, being too hot or cold for even a minute, even Bunji's milk being too runny or thick. If her pellets weren't normal after a day or two, then there was cause for concern. A trip to the vets meant a whole lot of unnecessary stress, which would then have flow-on effects.

As stress was the main risk to her wellbeing, we did our best to only visit the vet if it was truly necessary. Bunji didn't make it easy, though; as she began enjoying nibbling on things, she got adventurous. Once she took a chunk out of my hair while I was sleeping, and despite our best efforts, she sometimes managed a sneaky nibble of our wooden chairs. Luckily, she-oak almost always settled her stomach.

It was hard at times to keep things clean. As little joeys won't go to the toilet without help, they never really mess the pouch. As they develop and start to become comfortable going to the toilet on their own, though, it can become messy. Some wildlife carers have multiple pouches and pouch liners to swap out when others get dirty. This works great, but we didn't really have spares ... and as Bunji also liked to sleep with us, it became a little bit of a bedwetting issue.

On a whim, we decided to cut little tail-holes in some cute organic nappies we found, which allowed Bunji to go whenever she wanted without wetting the pouch or our bed. Bunji was so used to being handled by us that she didn't mind it at all when we put the nappies on her. We used this technique for a couple of months while she was spending a large amount of time in the pouch but going to the toilet by herself, and it made things so much easier.

I try to always make the most environmentally sustainable choices, but at the time, we hadn't even heard of reuseable nappies, and they weren't available in our local stores. Fortunately, in Bunji's case, nappies weren't something we were powering through; they were more of an occasional thing if we were camping or her other bedding was being washed. We didn't have to use too many of them, as it wasn't long before she started passing hard pellets.

The one thing most people don't tell you about wildlife care is that you do a *lot* of washing. Everything has to be clean, and washed only in natural products that won't harm the animals. Joeys go to the toilet multiple times a day, so those nappies saved us a lot of water!

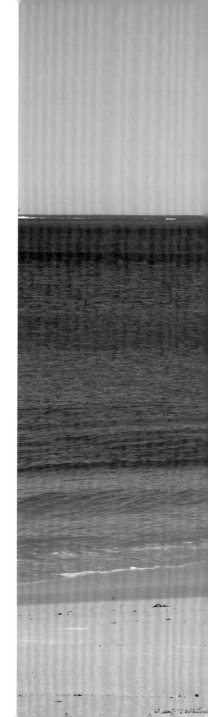

After a month or two of snacking on she-oak, Bunji started to try tumbling out of the pouch. At first she would have a little look around and quickly want to go back into her safe haven. We set up her pouch on a hanger that hung close to the ground, so if she did tumble out, she would simply roll onto the ground and not hurt herself. Bunji knew my voice, my smell – the first few times she ventured out, she stuck right by my side, her paws always hanging onto my hand. I was her safe place, and she slowly became more and more confident with being outside. I liked lying down with her on a picnic blanket in our backyard. One day, as we lay there, she fully rolled out and stood up on her wobbly little hind legs for the first time. It was a huge milestone.

There were many special moments in the early days of Bunji finding her feet. We spent a lot of time down at the local beaches across that summer. We liked to visit in the evening, when there was nobody around and the days were cooler. One evening in particular, we were sitting on the sand and watching the sunset. Bunji decided to climb out and hop around, so I took her on a little walk. She took brave little hops to follow me, and started scratching at my legs when she had enough. Watching her finding her feet and slowly getting more and more used to being out of the pouch brought me one of the strongest feelings of purpose I had ever felt.

To have this incredible little being that I was so connected to on every level be right by my side was unlike anything I had ever experienced. This relationship was so intimate and felt so natural; as every day went on, it made me realise how incredible these animals are, and how strong their bonds are with their mothers.

Not long after Bunji's first hops, I got a call from a friend of a friend. They had a few maremma-cross puppies that were only to be given away to the right homes. They were a one-off litter, one of those situations that doesn't really come up unless it is meant to be. It had been around six months since we lost Balu, and although I still had a hole in my heart, Bunji had helped me come to terms with it. We weren't knowingly going anywhere for some time, and my family would care for the dog in a heartbeat if something happened to me. I now had the opportunity to give another dog a beautiful life, and I badly wanted to give another pup a home.

Plus, I had a soft spot for the maremma breed. They're known for their loyalty, gentle nature and gorgeous personalities. Plus, they were livestock dogs that worked alongside sheep, chickens, even penguins; they protect, and they nurture. If I was to take on another dog while Bunji was around, it had to be placid, and gentle – like Balu. Basically, a maremma was perfect. So, I went and picked one up. I was immediately in love with a little girl left in the litter: a mix of maremma, border collie and heeler with muddled colours. She was ridiculously cute, even for a puppy – a tiny, gentle, little bundle of fluff that I just couldn't wait to show my world to. I named her 'Ohana', meaning 'family'; the months I had spent in Hawai'i meant I was familiar with a range of Hawai'ian words (and, of course, I loved *Lilo and Stitch*).

The journey of introducing a puppy into a household where there was already a larger-than-life personality like Bunji was so much fun. In the beginning stages, Ohana was wary of Bunji. Meanwhile, Bunji got very jealous of Ohana getting lots of attention. Over the first few weeks, they started to hang out, then follow each other and play. It was the sweetest thing to watch. Of course, in nature, a kangaroo's only natural predator is the native Australian dog, the dingo. You might think that Bunji and Ohana's friendship went against natural instincts, but funnily enough, it's quite a common occurrence for domestic dogs living on rural properties to become friendly with kangaroos. Bunji and Ohana became so comfortable with each other that they started sharing spaces even though they had the whole house to spread out in. They shared the dog bed, the bed in the Troopy carrier, even the towel down at the beach. (Bunji liked to dig little holes around Ohana, who would just roll around.)

They became really fond of each other's company, but also had a bit of a rivalry. Ohana would get jealous that Bunji got special little nut-and-seed mixes, and began copying Bunji, who would dig in her seed mix with her little paws and pick out the sunflower seeds. Ohana would use her nose to nudge away unwanted seeds or nuts, leaving the sunflower seeds behind. It was the same for any food Bunji got; if Bunji got a carrot, Ohana wanted a carrot. If Bunji got lettuce, Ohana wanted lettuce. Ohana developed a taste for fruit and vegetables that most dogs would never eat. As they grew, though, Bunji started getting bossier. Playtime was only on her terms, and she would hiss at Ohana if she was too close, or whack her on the head with her tiny little paws. One of the funniest things was watching Bunji play-attack Ohana's fluffy wagging tail, almost like a cat might.

Even though Bunji's paws were harmless, Ohana always respected her space and minded her own business. After all, Ohana's natural maremma instincts were to lie and observe – she was never a boisterous or overly energetic puppy, which suited Bunji just fine.

Ohana was always the first to let us know if Bunji was in a weird part of the house or yard, or if there was someone or something around. She had a huge vocal range and loved to use it, ranging from gentle whimpers to deep barks. When Bunji was up and about at night-time and it was disrupting her sleep, Ohana would do a tiny whimper, just loud enough to wake me up, and then lead me towards what was going on. She was incredibly smart and had a strong instinct to observe and protect. There was actually one Saturday night when I was home at Port Lincoln by myself with Ohana and Bunji and woke up to Ohana's very abrupt 'danger' bark at our front door. I had never heard her bark so loudly. It was about 2am, so I discreetly looked through my bedroom window curtains. About ten or fifteen very drunk men with bats and poles were trying to pick the lock of my front door. I was absolutely terrified. This was during a surge of gang activity in the area, but I had never thought I might be a target. Luckily, Ohana was barking so loudly that a few neighbours turned their lights on in their front yards; one even came out with his friend, waving a torch and yelling at the men. The men freaked out and ran off. I don't like thinking about what might have happened if Ohana hadn't been there. She saved me that night, and I trusted her with my life and Bunji's without hesitation.

It took a lot to faze Ohana. Once she was lying on the kitchen floor when a tiny mouse ran across the floor in front of her. It went back under the cupboard and then came back out, collecting crumbs not even a metre from Ohana's paws and head. Ohana watched curiously, but was unbothered. She wasn't a hunter or a chaser, she was a relaxer. Her calm, gentle nature was a blessing. As surfers, one of the key things we taught our dogs was to stay on the beach while we surfed. One of the first times I did this with Ohana, she was about twelve weeks old. It was a beautiful summer's day, and I left my clothes on my towel with some water under a beach umbrella. There were a few other surfer dogs lazing around, watching their owners catch the waves. I leant down, kissed Ohana, and said, 'You stay here, I'll be back.' She sat her paws down on my towel and, besides getting up every now and then to stretch, did not stray until I returned. She may have been part maremma, a breed known for loyalty and obedience, but it went beyond that. She always stayed by my side, and always followed my instructions. It was incomparable to anything I had ever seen in a dog before, let alone how she treated and loved Bunji. They were essentially adopted siblings.

This period of my time with Bunji was beautiful, but it was bittersweet. I knew it wouldn't last forever.

CHAPTER FIVE

Bunji leaves the nest

Animals should not require our permission to live on earth.
Animals were given the right to be here long before we arrived.

Anthony Douglas Williams

In South Australia, it's illegal to return hand-raised kangaroos to the wild. This is for a few reasons: it's difficult to hand-raise a joey to not be dependent on its human carer; and it's irresponsible to raise a joey without a mob or 'buddy' of their own, and then rerelease it into the wider world with no family unit – this can cause fatal amounts of stress. You can overcome the latter by buddying joeys together, essentially creating a family unit. Even then, transitioning the joeys from pouch life to soft release pens, and then from larger soft release pens to finally no pen at all, can take more than five years. Hand-raised kangaroos often don't wander too far from where they were rereleased, and in South Australia their chances of survival are low. Farmers usually hold legal permits to kill kangaroos, which they consider an agricultural 'pest'; you can only imagine what would happen if a hand-raised kangaroo trustingly hopped up to the wrong person. I wouldn't be returning Bunji to the wild. It would effectively be a death sentence.

With this in mind, it was really important to expose Bunji to potential emotional challenges from early on. This included unfamiliar sounds, tastes, people and animals, all of which are typical stressors for wild kangaroos. We knew that if she ended up at a sanctuary, it was likely that she would be around these things at some point, so the sooner she got used to them, the better. As we exposed her to the unfamiliar, she became unbothered by the loud sounds of cars, and dogs barking, and developed a strong immune system thanks to a wide range of different foods. She became resilient and calm in situations that would have stressed wild kangaroos out, and her confidence and curiosity only increased.

She even developed an obsession with the smell of curry after sneaking a bit that had dropped on the floor while I was cooking. I'm not sure what it was specifically that she liked about it, but whenever I was cooking vegetable curry, it was like having a tiny little velociraptor scraping at my legs. She would literally tumble out of her pouch and hop as fast as she could into the kitchen. Despite our best attempts, her strange tastes extended towards my boots, the table legs, my dress seams and even my hair. At this point, she wasn't snacking – just leaving a chewed-up trail of destruction.

Her curiosity and confidence carried beyond food. One day, when we were set up camping somewhere between Port Lincoln and Streaky Bay, it was a hot summer's day, and Ty and I were taking turns having little dips in the lagoon. Bunji was bigger now, and pretty confident being out of the pouch. She liked testing the edge of her personal boundaries; she'd go for a quick hop a little way from me, but then come right back to hover at my feet. On that day, I had walked down to the beach with Ohana and Bunji following close behind. I wondered, *if I swim, will Bunji just wait on the beach?*

I wasn't sure what Bunji thought of salt water; she loved being in the shower with us, and drank from taps and water bowls. She seemed to like bodies of water, but the shower was a little different to the ocean.

I walked slowly into the water. Ohana followed, and then Bunji: ankle-deep, then shin-deep, then waist-deep. Bunji took two huge leaps into the water, so much deeper than she could stand – and then she started paddling with her little paws! I knew kangaroos could swim, but to see Bunji just take to the water like a fish was incredible. She paddled around in the shallows for a few moments before hopping out.

She shook off, licked her paws, then waited for me. It was truly incredible.

On another memorable trip to Esperance, Bunji also came with us. I had been offered a job with Tourism Australia as talent in a campaign that three good friends of mine were photographing. The trip involved camping, beach days, and exploring national parks; Bunji was at a stage where she was healthy, strong, loved long walks, and was still hanging out in her pouch, so we decided to take her. Not only would the trip be amazing for her, but Bunji hadn't yet been introduced to any other carers that she trusted or felt comfortable with. New people can cause terrible stress on kangaroos, but I was Bunji's safe space, so she was coming with us.

With a packed car, a swag and all the gear we needed for Bunji, we made our way up and over the spellbinding Nullarbor Plain, right around the iconic Great Australian Bight. The Bight is a place of unparalleled natural beauty, home to one of the most amazing marine environments on the planet. We needn't have worried about how Bunji would react to my friends; she was as taken with them as they were with her.

On one of the days, we lay on a beach under an umbrella in the national park, just chatting and enjoying ourselves. Bunji stretched out, halfway out of her pouch on the sun-warmed rug. I remember thinking, *this is like something out of a movie*. It was such a wonderful, peaceful moment surrounded by those I loved – a memory I'll treasure forever. That same night, we went to another beach for the sunset. Bunji loves stretching her little legs on the beach, so Ty and I let her out of her pouch and went for a little jog. She followed ever so closely behind, and was clearly having the time of her life.

When she had enough, she put her paws on my legs as if to say, 'Put me in the pouch now, please,' and that was that. We even hiked up to the top of a mountain lookout with her in her pouch. I remember watching her looking out over the landscape and thinking to myself how incredible her species is.

When we arrived back in Port Lincoln, we felt like we had come home with a beautiful young kangaroo rather than a cute little joey. Bunji had become so confident and comfortable with getting in and out of the pouch by herself, was happily chewing on solids, and enjoyed lazing around on the dog bed, lounge or in front of our heater. She was happy to spend time in our yard, grazing on grass and she-oak, digging little holes and starting to make literal leaps and bounds towards becoming a grown kangaroo.

I always knew that there would come a time when I would need to make a serious plan for Bunji. I was happy to sacrifice my time and career to give her the best home she could have, but I also knew that transitioning her to somewhere that she could safely roam was something I needed to start searching for. My dream would have been to own hundreds of acres, somewhere I could live while caring for Bunji and other rescue animals without having to worry about space or safety. Being in my early twenties, though, I knew it wasn't a reality. I was at the start of my career – I was getting opportunities thrown at me every month for amazing trips, partnerships and to be a part of other conservation work and projects. If I was able to find a place where she would be happy without me, I could help many more animals. It tore my heart in two even thinking about leaving her, but I knew that time was going to come.

Bunji was over a year old by this point, and I needed to put concrete plans in place for the future. Finding kangaroo carers was hard, and finding a sanctuary I agreed with was even harder. It needed to be someone's home, someone with the right set-up and the right mindset, someone who would be committed to her forever. I started reaching out to the wildlife community and telling people about Bunji's story and our special bond. It took a while – Ty and I checked out quite a few places – and then we met Bronte and Linda.

They were an amazing couple that I found through friends of friends. I was having trouble finding anyone who had the space and set-up to care for Bunji. Somebody gave me Linda's contact information – just a name and number. It wasn't much to work with, but I gave her a call and explained the situation. Taking on a Euro is a big ask, but out of the handful of people I had chatted to, Linda was the first to show any interest. Linda and Bronte lived on a neary ten-acre property called 'Two Songs', and shared our deep love for kangaroos. Their property was already home to three other rescue kangaroos, and was partially fenced with Colorbond fencing. Colorbond fencing is important for caring for kangaroos; it's strong, chew-safe and opaque, meaning that kangaroos can't be spooked by the sight of roaming wildlife, cars or people. It also means that if they do get spooked and run, they won't be severely injured if they hit the fence; it's tragically common for spooked kangaroos to run into wire fencing and strangle themselves to death, known as 'fence hanging'.

The Colorbond fencing was a good sign that Linda and Bronte were serious about their animals.

We visited, and met their other rescues – all red kangaroos, named Eric, Maloo and Imogen. Their property seemed like the perfect forever home for Bunji. It was beautiful, peaceful and spacious, but not so big that Bunji would feel scared. It was a new project for Linda and Bronte; they had big plans for more animals, more trees, and a separate enclosure in case they got in other animals such as wombats.

I was a very passionate, confident and new-age–minded young person when it came to wildlife care and conservation. Although we were from different backgrounds and walks of life, the first day that I met Linda and Bronte I knew we would become really good friends. At first, Linda and Bronte were understandably hesitant to take on another roo joey; it's a huge responsibility. Luckily, they agreed that over the next few months, we would start taking Bunji to visit their property, let her adjust to it and them, and see how she would go. Bunji was used to seeing a fence and used to having her zone, so we just set up a little area using corrugated iron and added a wood shelter with hay, all of her favourite toys and blankets. That was the beginning of her first visit to Two Songs.

By then, many carers had said to me, 'You're going to struggle to transition Bunji' and 'She's yours for life.' Although I already knew the bond between Bunji and I was strong, our first few visits to Two Songs put it in a whole new light.

One of the main reasons we kept Bunji on the bottle was to make her comfortable with someone who wasn't me or Ty feeding her. Bunji was very much dependent on me. Although she had a bond with Ty, it became more and more apparent as time went on that her attachment to me as time went on was her priority. So, on the first few visits, we took Bunji in while she was still inside her pouch, and set her up in her shelter. I spent a lot of time lying there in the hay with her while she got used to the new surroundings, voices, and smells. We introduced her to Linda and Bronte, but it was me and Ty or no one. This was something I had expected, and also something that I expected to slowly change over time.

Our first priority was to get other people feeding Bunji. This wasn't too difficult, because Bunji went into a happy little daze when feeding. So, when her eyes closed, I simply handed the bottle to Bronte or Linda. Bunji wouldn't open her eyes until she was done feeding. When she opened her eyes and realised a stranger was feeding her, she initially let go and hopped back to her little safe zone or to me. After the first few visits, we successfully got Bunji to accept Bronte or Linda giving her the bottle. This was step one. It was slow progress, but it was still progress. She was also pretty used to Two Songs and all of its sounds at this point, so things were looking good.

The next step was the hardest: getting Bunji comfortable being there without me. We started off visiting three times a week. I would hang out with Bunji for a while, and then leave for an hour or two. But once I got Bunji all comfy in her shelter, she would still follow me when I got up to walk to the gate, right by my feet. As I closed the gate, she tried to come out, clicking and making the 'shh shh' noises she always made – the natural signal for her mum.

The first time I did this, I felt awful leaving her there, like my heart was breaking. I imagine it feeling like when a mother drops her child off at day-care for the first time. I felt like I was abandoning her, leaving a piece of myself behind. Bunji felt the same way, clearly. I had to take a few deep breaths. This was the hardest part, but it was also needed, and it was going to get easier. I walked back in the gate, crouching down to cuddle Bunji to let her know everything was fine, talking to her like I always did. I told her, and myself, that she was completely safe there, and this was for the best. I kissed her, and then stood up, walked out the gate and drove off.

Of course, I was on the phone to Linda and Bronte only minutes later. 'How is she going? What is she doing? Has she settled?' (Another thing I feel might be an experience mothers can relate to!) For the entirety of the first three times I left her there, they told me that Bunji didn't leave the gate or fence until I returned a few hours later. This really hurt. I loved her so much, but she *had* to get used to being here. Thankfully, after the first month, Bunji started exploring her surroundings during the visits. She hopped around, sniffed the other kangaroos, and allowed Bronte in particular to feed her. This was a huge relief for me. I badly wanted her to form a bond with Linda or Bronte in the early days so that she learnt that it was also home, and we still had a long way to go.

Over the next few months, we slowly worked on increasing the length of Bunji's visits, then having her first overnight stays (accompanied by me at first), then staying for full days, nights and weekends. Both Linda and Bronte put in huge amounts of effort to make Bunji feel at home, and Bunji really took to Bronte in particular.

She was spoiled at Two Songs, just like she was with us, and her personality at the sanctuary shone bright. She was the smallest out of the rescued kangaroos there, but had the biggest amount of confidence. Not easily intimidated, she would chase the other roos away from a fresh batch of sweet potatoes, and she found her happy, quiet little places around the property by herself. We worked up to leaving her there for a week before coming back.

That was a stressful week for me. I worried mostly about her being upset by not seeing me for that long. Linda and Bronte had told me she went through phases when I left her there; she went between being happy doing her own thing to looking a little lost and sniffing along the fence line, and that week was no different. I had to remind myself that she would take a long time to get used to me not being around. Most importantly, she was otherwise fine – not stressed at all.

After five months of this, Bunji was spending hardly any time in the pouch, and being on the move with her was more difficult than when she was a joey. Between this and our concern that taking her to and from Two Songs was becoming counterproductive to her transition, we decided it was time for Two Songs to be Bunji's new home. It was a huge milestone after a long journey that still had some bumps in the road to cross, but the hardest part was over. Besides – we could visit as often as we wanted!

CHAPTER SIX

Bunji's new family

There may be times when we feel powerless to prevent injustice, but there must never be a time when we fail to protest.

Elie Wiesel

Seeing how Linda and Bronte ran Two Songs reignited my interest in beginning a larger-scale project, an idea that I had been toying with for some time. I had always wanted to start my own organisation, ever since I first got into animal care and conservation. I had come across so many issues over the years that I felt needed a voice.

I found that I didn't always agree with the discourse or processes in the conservation world. In Australia especially, many conservation charities still running had started in the 1970s and 1980s. Their messaging was outdated, pushing the blame for ecosystem collapse to animals rather than the humanity's impact of humanity. After so many years working and volunteering in marine conservation, wildlife rescue and wildlife conservation, and seeing how charities can do great work or be ineffective, I wanted to start my own foundation. I was tired of seeing so many issues not being addressed properly, or solutions being brought to light because of people's outdated mindsets. Like the fact that kangaroos are not a pest, but have been deemed as such by the agricultural industry because they are competitors for land. Many commercial fisheries have done the same to sea lions, and seals because these animals took crayfish out of their pots, or salmon out of the farms. I was tired of old-fashioned thinking being at the forefront of the laws in place for how we treat wildlife. Even the more progressive wildlife conservation organisations I volunteered for hit governmental red tape where they 'couldn't overcome' issues such as addressing the use of 1080 baits and the suffering they cause.

I felt like we needed an entirely new way of doing things. The only way I could help, raise awareness and begin upheaving how we approach conservation was by starting from scratch and growing a community of like-minded people. I brainstormed for a long time on the name, and I landed on Balu Blue.

To me, Balu Blue represented everything I wanted to change in addition to the values I wanted to promote. 'Balu' for my beautiful dog who lost his life thanks to the government's disinterest in banning an incredibly dangerous and toxic poison (proven time and time again to be ineffective, cruel and nonselective) in favour of prioritising agricultural profits over habitat protection for our wildlife. 'Blue' for our planet, made up of 71 per cent water, and also for my background in marine conservation. The name felt like a perfect representation of my drive to do something real and long-lasting.

Of course, in reality starting a charity with only a handful of help is no simple feat. It became more and more daunting the deeper I dived into it. There was so much involved: constitutions, boards, minutes, meetings, lawyers, accountants. The list went on, and I wasn't interested in any of it! I just wanted to speak up for our wildlife, cover some costs so we could rescue more animals, and run beach clean-ups to get leftover fishing lines off the local beaches in Port Lincoln. Frustrated, I worked my way through checking off the required boxes, and in the meantime, started putting together groups and events on Facebook for a beach clean-up with a matching hashtag. This was Balu Blue's first real 'event', and to my surprise it grabbed a bit of online momentum. My brain sped off into a vortex of what we could one day achieve, and I had to remind myself it was one step at a time.

I also organised to screen the recently released documentary *Before the Flood*, featuring Leonardo DiCaprio, on Port Lincoln's main street. I hired a refrigerator truck to be parked on the lawn, and also hired a projector. We decked out the grass area with bean bags, rugs and cushions, and made it a free event. *Before the Flood* is narrated by Leo as he talks with world leaders, scientists and activists, and shows harrowing footage of what we are doing to our planet. The fact that Leonardo DiCaprio was in it helped gloss over my being a 20-something woman showing a doco about environmental destruction in a town built on wheat, sheep and fish farming. Around 100 to 150 people rocked up to watch it, which for me was a win. That was 150 people who went home thinking about what they were contributing to and how they could change to help ensure a future for our planet and our children.

Balu Blue's growth was also helped by my social media presence. I had a pretty good following from my years of surfing, work and (of course) posting cute pictures of Bunji and Ohana. More and more people wanted to get involved helping us achieve our goals – one of which was, at that time, to help upgrade Two Songs.

In 2017, a while after Bunji had properly moved in there, Linda, Bronte and I were brainstorming how we could work together to raise funds to turn Two Songs into an accredited sanctuary. Caring for wildlife is not a cheap activity – the milk replacements alone are incredibly expensive. What I've learnt over the years is that most wildlife carers just do it off their own back, often putting the animal's health and wellbeing before their own. Adding Bunji to the animals at their property meant Linda and Bronte's costs had risen significantly. Linda and Bronte privately owned their property, and were not a charity as such; but because Balu Blue Foundation was a registered charity, we could raise funds to support them.

Over the next few years, proceeds from Balu Blue helped cover costs such as veterinary bills, food, fencing and dirt for new enclosures. Linda and Bronte had put in so much work already but had a specific goal to put up several Colorbond fences across the entire property – not just the paddock – to create new enclosures for the animals. We started brainstorming ways that we could help. That spring, my community stepped in; I received a message from three girls in Western Australia, who had been following Bunji's journey on my social media. Their names were Nush, Kaity and Taylor, and they wanted to ride 2600 kilometres on their bicycles to raise the funds for the fence. I spoke to them on the phone, and they were three of the loveliest people I'd had a chance to talk to in a while: full of life, energy and excitement. I was thrilled. What an amazing goal, adventure and purpose! After that phone call, they started a fundraiser online. In a short few months and with a lot of promoting from all four of us, we managed to raise $5400 to go towards the fence through Balu Blue.

Nush, Taylor and Kaity rode their bikes from Perth, Western Australia to Port Lincoln, South Australia, facing all the weather that the Great Australian Bight threw at them along the way. They rode across the Nullarbor, which includes Australia's longest straight road: the 90-mile straight. They travelled through some of the harshest landscapes in Australia, all while sharing the road with semitrailers. It was a huge feat. When the girls arrived in Port Lincoln, they looked incredible considering what they had just achieved and despite their exhaustion and bruises. They stayed at our house, and over the following days Ty and I took them to Two Songs to show them what they would be supporting. The girls got to meet Linda, Bronte, Bunji and all the rescue animals there; it was such a beautiful moment, and I treasured the new friendships that came from working together for a great cause. The girls headed off soon after – happily, in a car this time – and we promised to see each other soon.

Linda and Bronte got to work right away on quoting up earthworks, fencing and the rest. It gave me great fulfillment to know Balu Blue had been a part of the beginning of such a great forever home for many animals to come.

Not too long after the new fence was finished, Bunji had well and truly settled in. She had completely gotten used to the property, Bronte, Linda and the other kangaroos. I visited her regularly. It made me so happy to see her settled in, but at the same time, I greatly missed her in my day-to-day life. She had been a part of it for two years, and I felt like something was missing with her at Two Songs.

It seemed Bunji felt the same; Linda and Bronte couldn't help but notice her solidarity from the other kangaroos. All the grey or red kangaroos would lounge around together, but Bunji would hop off and find her own space. While it's typical of Euro kangaroos to value alone time, that's only true when surrounded by kangaroos of other species. Linda, Bronte and I wondered: if Bunji had a Euro buddy, would she choose to hang out with it?

Not long after our discussion about this came a boy named George. Sadly, most joeys handed in to wildlife carers in rural South Australia are orphaned from shootings, not car accidents. George fell into this category. His mum had been shot, and one of the bullets had gone through her pouch while little joey George was still inside. The bullet had taken off George's left hind foot, but he had somehow survived. When a kangaroo's hind legs are injured, they are often unable to balance or walk at all, resulting in euthanasia. Luckily, George still had his elbow and a tiny inch or two of foot left for balance. George's hops were more of a crawl, but aside from this, he made a return to good health and still had a great quality of life. Linda and Bronte decided to take on George with the aim of making him Bunji's companion. Both Euro kangaroos could become friends, and keep each other company.

When George came along, it was clear that he and Bunji knew that they were the same species; they took an immediate interest in each other, rather than in the other roos. George was a lot more keen on being Bunji's friend than the other way around, though. Bunji, ever the lone wolf, would usually go and curl up under the grass or a tree at the bottom of the paddock and mind her own business. George was determined to befriend her, sniffing and hanging around her. Sometimes she didn't take too kindly to it – Linda and Bronte often told me stories of Bunji being not so nice to George when his offers of friendship got a bit annoying. Bunji was used to her previous friend, Ohana, being a bit more respectful of her personal space.

George won her over, though. Each time I came to visit, I noticed them spending more and more time together, lying down in the middle of the paddock. Of course, Bunji was still the boss; where Bunji went, George followed. After a few months, they had become each other's closest friends. They slept, rested and ate together.

I think George even understood that I was Bunji's special person – he would always come and say hello when Bunji did, rather than shying away from me, a stranger. It made us so happy to see the bond developing between them. Bunji now had a buddy, and George, who overcame all odds, had a friend and a safe sanctuary to live out his days in peace. It was a success.

CHAPTER SEVEN

Raising $500,000 for the bushfires

You are personally responsible for becoming more ethical than the society you grew up in.

Eliezer Yudkowsky

The year to follow was one of life-altering opportunities and growth for me, starting with me and Ty separating and going our separate ways. It was a time to check in with myself; I knew I was ready to shift my focus back to my career. This shift involved making the choice to move to Western Australia, where I longed to be for many reasons: the Ningaloo Reef had become a second home to me; I had great friends and a variety of work opportunities there. Not to mention, the ocean drew me back on its own each time I went. I could see myself settling down there.

Although I had built a life in Port Lincoln and on the Eyre Peninsula, and had so many beautiful friends and family close by, I had big dreams and big plans. The choice to move away from Bunji in particular was really hard, because unlike my family and friends, I couldn't just call her up when I missed her. The knowledge that Two Songs was her home and that she was comfortable and safe there made me feel a lot better. Besides, I knew I would be visiting regularly.

So, I found myself a shed house on acreage to lease on the Exmouth Gulf. I had been nervous about the move, but I was also thrilled to arrive. I found two housemates to help share the living costs with. Just like that, six months flew by in my new home. I still came back to South Australia pretty regularly, and visited Bunji every single time. I had worried she would forget me, or that our bond would lessen, but I didn't need to be afraid. The first time I visited after moving, she immediately ran up and cuddled me. She hung around for a while, and then went off to lie in the paddock with George. It was like she knew I was visiting – that I wasn't gone forever – but that she also was happy with her day-to-day life at Two Songs. That independence gave me huge peace of mind; I had made the right choice for both of us.

At the end of winter, I was offered a unique role as a professional freediver on a Tourism Indonesia shoot, which would see me spend four weeks in remote Indonesia, with three videographers and photographers. I had no idea of the path that would follow once I took this job. I quit my job on the whale shark boat, and asked my friends to house-sit for me and take care of Ohana. And just like that, I was off.

I was about to be the only person in front of a camera at some crazy places; we visited locations inaccessible to the general public and where foreigners hadn't ever stepped foot. We travelled with a local Indonesian team, making many overnight journeys on tiny wooden boats full of pelican cases of camera gear to reach the location by morning, using each other's shoulders as pillows.

There were so many cool experiences on this trip: dragging my hand through bioluminescent water during a midnight boat trip, freediving with whale sharks off the coast of Borneo, modelling in an underwater photoshoot in a crystal-clear lake full of stingless jellyfish. It was the most fulfilled and exhausted I had ever felt. Being part of the campaign also really made it clear to me that Balu Blue needed more sponsorship to do bigger and better things.

Not long after this, I started working with sponsors again – this time not only for my surfing and freediving, but also to be part of wildlife conservation projects all over the world. This took me to India, where I filmed and shared the stories of wildlife suffering in the entertainment industry and being rescued. I went to Africa and learnt about antipoaching movements and the battles that the wildlife there faces as I bathed rescued elephants. I did some travelling at home too, heading to the Kimberley with local guides to photograph the scenery in all its glory. learnt from local Elders how to safely eat from the bush. While I was there, I met a lady in Kununurra who had rescued and rehabilitated hundreds of animals in need, mostly on her own – an incomprehensible level of impact, all from just one person! I absorbed everything around me, sharing my passions with so many on my journey, and then got to take all of it home with me.

My travels cemented what I already knew was at the forefront of the issues facing wildlife: the general population's lack of education and awareness. These two issues would be Balu Blue's first and foremost focus. I was also thinking about Balu Blue's overall attitude to conservation and how I wanted it to be different to other organisations.

My goal was to approach conservation with a mindset that was up-to-date with how our natural world has been impacted by humanity on a wide scale, usually because of our own greed as a species. I wanted Balu Blue to focus on whole ecosystem restoration, and I wanted to continue building our kind, inclusive community that shared my goal of a kinder future in which we were living and sharing our land with nature. I wanted to help build a generation that isn't scared to make changes to systems that have been broken for decades and harmful to our wild places. I was one person, but I knew I could make serious change. Bunji was proof.

I did my best to visit South Australia as often as possible, but between my travels and running Balu Blue, time got away from me. At one point, I didn't see Bunji for eight months, the longest period of time that we had been away from each other yet. When I finally arrived at Two Songs, I had the hugest lump in my stomach from excitement.

I walked down into the paddock, called out 'Bunji' – and my little girl immediately came out of the bushes at the bottom of the large paddock. Even from a distance it was so obvious that it was her: the way she hops, her little white patch on her back. She came straight up to me. I leant down and she pressed her head into mine, grabbing onto my hands, hugging me like she used to. I cried a little bit, getting a few tears in her fur. *Surely,* I thought, *this is how it feels when someone hasn't seen their child in a long, long time.* Once I gathered myself, we spent some time just hanging out. She'd cuddle for a bit, her paw on my leg or foot, then go off to munch on some grass before coming back for another cuddle.

Despite having lived at Two Songs for over two years and seeing me once every few months at best, she still had this bond with me – and only me. Linda and Bronte confirmed this as I caught up with them; she didn't come up to anyone else like that. The love that we share with these animals is truly a forever kind of love. It was a bright moment in what had been a rewarding but also challenging time for me – it fortified me, something that I would desperately need not too long after I returned home.

The end of 2019 saw the start of what I recall as the worst natural disaster of my lifetime and, to my knowledge, in Australia's bushfire history. I was over on Yorke Peninsula, visiting and staying with my dad; when my parents separated over a decade ago, he moved into our holiday house in Marion Bay, bordered by national parkland and farms. It was only twenty kilometres from Kangaroo Island, a place we had visited during many family holidays. As kids, we had always gone through heat waves; South Australian summers were really hot, and 40°C was normal. But this summer on the Yorke Peninsula, the heat waves were drawn out and the land was bone dry.

The typical summer fires started burning all around South Australia, and then all over New South Wales and Victoria. Fires have always scared me more than anything else in the natural world. Their ability to completely destroy an entire region is terrifying. I remember one time when I was a kid that a wildfire was only a kilometre or two from our home. The wind changed in our favour, saving our house, but I'll never forget driving to safety on a country road lined with trees ablaze.

These fires burning now were more intense than in the past, and pretty much every small town on the Yorke Peninsula was on stand-by for evacuation. All I could think about were all the animals trapped on Kangaroo Island. I started reaching out to everyone that I knew, trying to come up with a way to evacuate the wildlife there. Within two to three days, the Kangaroo Island fires were out of control. It was like a horror movie. From the beach near Dad's, I could see a cloud over the island, like nothing I had ever witnessed before; the fire was so hot it had created its own atmosphere. We had friends over there working as firefighters, and they told us there was nothing they could do: the fire was just too intense. It was burning everything, ground to sky. The animals that made it out alive were fleeing to the ocean.

My heart shattered as I helplessly watched the landscape and the wildlife I grew up with die. Luckily the fire missed us on Yorke Peninsula, and also missed Two Songs – but it had burnt areas that were far too close for comfort. These fires were hotter and more aggressive than anything in history. This was the true impact of climate change. I saw photos from my followers in other areas where the fires were burning as bad as Kangaroo Island, and photos of families in their boats in the bay as their houses and the towns they knew and loved went up in flames. When the fires cooled enough for fire crews to get in and assess the damage, it was utterly devastating. I struggled not to fall into a heap of tears; so much of the places I loved had been destroyed. I can only imagine how people who lost their homes and loved ones felt, and with this in mind, I decided to use my platform to help.

Over the next 48 hours, I put together videos, photos and other posts, directing people who wanted to send funds to a number of different areas: wildlife rescues, firefighters, donation pools for people who had lost their houses. The list felt endless, but to my surprise, I reached millions of people over the first week or so. It was amazing to see so many people offering help, but I wanted to ensure the funds weren't all going to just one place. Luckily, my friends Jake and Marie reached out to me on Instagram, as they were starting a fundraiser called Influence For Good. The funds would go to rescues and organisations that weren't receiving funds from the larger fundraisers at the time, but had still lost everything and needed to rebuild. I got together with five other people with a following on Instagram or YouTube and collaboratively we raised approximately $500,000. It was enough to donate to six different charities and causes, and would help a lot of people and animals. I was chatting to so many different wildlife carers as well as my fellow fundraisers, trying to gauge how we could divide the money between both humanitarian and animal causes. At the time, Celeste Barber and a few other celebrities were running online fundraisers that raised millions, but the chosen recipients were largely based in New South Wales. The smaller rescue groups in other states that were burning, including South Australia and Victoria, wouldn't receive anything. We decided to help fill those gaps.

The funds went to firefighters in South Australia and Victoria, to organisations providing aid to those who had lost everything in the fires and were homeless, to Wildlife Victoria, to bat clinics and various smaller animal rescues based in South Australia and Victoria, and to Balu Blue. The donations to Balu Blue meant that we could support the smaller, non-official charities or carers that we knew personally who desperately needed help not just in that moment, but for what would be the hard year to follow.

This was the first time Balu Blue was actually able to provide a significant amount to organisations in need. We were able to immediately send support money to carers across Australia who were in dire straits, and it also meant we could start considering larger projects in the future – though that would have to wait. The aftermath of the fires was truly daunting. I decided to go back to Adelaide so that I could help with some of the rescue efforts going on in the Adelaide Hills, which had been hit hard.

My mum is a huge animal lover and accompanied me to a few separate koala rescues that we had been driving funds to over the course of the fires. The scenes were unbelievable: hundreds of koalas filled up a school gym, huddled in clumps, as hundreds of volunteers helped care for them. It was an incredible effort. Mum and I accompanied the crew on rescue efforts to check the burnt forest areas for koalas that needed help.

Koalas climb trees when they are in danger. It's an instinct that horribly backfires during a bushfire, and so many of the koalas we found had burnt to death as they sat in the branches. The abundant forests that were once loud with birdsong were hauntingly silent as we retrieved these poor koalas. Some of the rescuers from the team had been out there days prior, euthanising countless injured animals that had no chance of survival. I really struggled; seeing so much loss of life was incredibly traumatic, and left images living in my head for a long time.

It wasn't all bad, though. Mum and I also met many of the survivors, largely baby koalas that had lost their mums and adult koalas with minor burns. We helped release two koalas into a gum-rich property that backed onto a winery in the Adelaide Hills, and though it was a small thing to see them free to start a new life, it gave me hope. These times were hard for so many people. Not only those who lost everything in the fires, but those who dropped everything for weeks to help others who needed it. I didn't think about any other part of my life for about a month; it consumed me. There have been times in my life where my passion for something happening in the moment just naturally takes over, and looking after myself during those times is something I still feel like I'm working on. I was around my family during the fires, and tried to take a break now and then by surfing, but it was pretty hard to put my mind elsewhere. There was just so much to do. I was very much a messenger for a lot of people, which then led to people leaning on me for advice, and then to me organising further rescue situations. At the end of each day, I had to remind myself I was just one person, and I was doing all I could. Eventually, things started getting a bit better, and I could take a breath.

As things calmed down a little, I could think about the long-term again. One of the main goals I had when starting Balu Blue was to one day buy or support land for a protected reserve, whether it be for native wildlife or other rescued animals in need. An overwhelming number of animal lives had been lost in the fires, but more than that: the survivors' habitats were entirely gone. It would take years for those areas to heal. I urgently wanted to ensure that Australia's remaining habitats were being protected. My worry was that after all of these animals had faced the worst fires in Australian history, they would then go on to face the usual battles in the few remaining habitat areas, such as hunting, poison, clearing, logging and pollution.

The roadblock to acquiring land or embarking on a larger rescue project was funding, something that would take a long time to gather. While Balu Blue worked towards that, I would have to think outside the box, and keep developing my career.

I'd established myself as a sponsored freediver by then, and also stepped back into the pro-surfing world as an environmentalist, able to tell my stories and inspire a kinder path for an industry that heavily relies on the ocean as its canvas. I spent most of my time in the ocean and with that came so many scenarios that drove my passions for wanting to help marine life, and all wildlife. Balu Blue worked on cutting fishing line off sharks on dives and disentangling seabirds and turtles from rubbish.

I also diversified my income streams in the form of two businesses. There is Bandicoot, a jewellery line I founded selling small keepsakes representing the sea, made from quality materials and ethically made by people I personally know. A percentage of profits goes back to Balu Blue to support our work. Then there is my expeditions business, which came from converting my experiences working as a freediver for brands and companies into a business that allows my online community to come on educational, life-altering journeys with wildlife in the wild. I have taken people freediving with humpback whales in Tonga, kayaking with whales in between icebergs in Antarctica, and got them working hands-on with the best rescue sanctuaries in South Africa to help the rhino poaching crisis. My initial career goals had come to life, and with that all set in motion and growing each year, my goal to grow my foundation was rising higher and higher. I didn't know how my life could be any richer – but then I fell in love.

CHAPTER EIGHT

Love, life and death in Tasmania

The goal of life is to make your heartbeat match the beat of
the universe, to match your nature with Nature.

Joseph Campbell

I had known Chippa for quite a long time. He's an extremely talented pro surfer, so we had a few mutual friends and followed each other on our socials. He was curious about my work with animals and my travels, and we had chatted a few times across the years – but we had never met in person. Our conversations picked up though as he followed my fundraising efforts for the fires, and by the time I returned to my pre-fire life, we were chatting pretty much every day through a mixture of texts, voice notes and Facetimes. We wanted to meet in person, but we couldn't get the times to line up. The only time we were going to be in the same place was when we would both be passing through Sydney Airport
– so we decided to make it work.

I was flying to the Philippines, about to host my first ever freedive trip with paying customers; Chippa was on his way to America. Chippa had only twenty minutes to spare between flights, so he told me to order him a coffee while he caught a taxi from the domestic terminal over to the international terminal. I was so nervous as I sat there, waiting for him to walk around the corner. I shouldn't have worried; we immediately clicked.

Meeting in person for the first time was surreal. We were unusually comfortable after the initial nerves wore off, talking about so many things. He wasn't at all intimidated by my passion and determination to change things with Balu Blue, and he clearly shared the same values as me. He was kind, humble and confident. I couldn't stop staring at his eyes. I was in awe of them. It was just pure happiness that I felt in that tiny bit of time we had together. Those twenty minutes went far too quickly, and we hugged goodbye before he rushed back to his gate.

In the weeks following, our time zones made it difficult to carry out conversation by text or organise voice calls. We ended up sending each other voice notes, which was new to me but nice. It felt more personal, a lot more intimate, than a text message. About four weeks after we met at the airport, we decided that this thing between us was going to be very real. We made a plan for the very beginning of March. I had been asked to attend a weekend sustainability event for Virgin Australia Airlines in Melbourne. Meanwhile, Chippa happened to be flying back around the same time. I told him to meet me in Melbourne; Virgin had put me up in a hotel room for two nights, so he could hang with me there and we could chat about what we would do next.

When I arrived in Melbourne, I couldn't wait to see him. Chippa's eighteen-hour flight got into Melbourne at 5am, and as if I'd known him for my entire life, I told him to just come into my room and go to sleep. I figured, why not? I would already be asleep, so I left a key at reception for him. I woke up to find him next to me, sleeping fully clothed and over the covers. This being the second time we met in real life was, again, quite surreal.

We got a coffee before I went to my event, and after that we hung out in a totally foreign place just cruising around, eating, and lying on the grass. It's still one of my most favourite days. I felt we were both on the exact same wavelength in a way that I'd never had before. Before we left, we figured out what to do next: he would come to Western Australia in the coming weeks so we could spend some more time together. He was living down in Tasmania at the time, but had some free time between surf trips. From there, we could navigate how we could continue to see each other. We were so excited – but, like everyone else in the world, our plans were about to change. COVID-19 hit Australia, and we went into lockdown.

I thought, *of course I finally meet 'the one' right as the world locks us away from each other.* What followed between us was many letters, Facetimes, planning and good old reassurances that this was it – that from now on, we were a team, no matter what. Part of the problem was Western Australia's intense lockdown laws for incoming travellers, who had to apply for what was essentially a domestic visa. We finally got to see each other again after six months when Chippa's visa was approved, and from there it was leaps forward together.

This included adding another furry member to our family: Rain, a border collie puppy from a litter in Esperance. My friend Lisa had a loving border collie called Phoenix, who came into her life from a not-so-loving farm near Esperance. Lisa had allowed Phoenix to have one litter of puppies with a neighbour's border collie before he was fixed, and I was one of the first to be told.

Ohana was my constant companion through those six months of lockdown. I thought it would be nice for her to have a doggy friend for when Chippa and I went to places we couldn't take her.

Though it had been in my mind for a while to get Ohana a friend, I hadn't started actively looking through adoption and rescue pages when Lisa reached out. Chippa and I decided to get one of the puppies, and called her Rain. I'll never forget when we put Rain into the back seat of the Hilux that first day. Ohana was in shock, ever-so-gently sniffing her as if Rain was her own puppy. Maybe Ohana missed Bunji, or maybe it was just her maremma instincts, but Rain's addition to the family filled her with new purpose. They have been best friends ever since.

After spending the year up north in Western Australia, Chippa and I decided to spend some time at the place Chippa had called home base for the last five years: North-East Tasmania. Chippa had gone above and beyond to make it to Western Australia during the lockdowns, and I didn't want him to feel homesick. Plus, I was so excited to just be with Chippa and I knew we would be doing a lot of back and forth in the following years. I was excited to see his life down there, to see the place he had called home. I was also pretty keen to have our own space after living in a share house for so many years.

It was, however, bittersweet – mostly because I was in love with the life I had built up in Western Australia. My friends were close by and good diving and waves were right at my doorstep, but I had to trust that life would take us in the right direction. Besides, we planned to come back to West Oz in the long-term. It was time for something new.

I'd never been to Tasmania before, and although I had a fair idea of what it was like, nothing prepared me for its beauty: huge, temperate forests with giant ferns; the clearest and cleanest water I've ever drank; freezing crisp air blowing off the Antarctic; and the blue, crystal-clear ocean that, during a storm, turned into the wildest sea I had ever seen.

Despite all this beauty, in the first month I found it hard to steer my concentration away from the sheer amount of wildlife that was hit on the roads. It was astounding and horrible.

Thanks to the harsh cold and wind, especially in wintertime, the wildlife in Tasmania was fluffier and smaller than its mainland cousins. There were multiple species of wallabies, such as the pademelon (one of the cutest things you'll ever see), plenty of thick-coated wombats, echidnas marching around in train-like formations, and brushtail possums always out seeking moths and ants that are on the roads at night-time. Among the most fascinating animals are the quolls. Tasmania has two species: the eastern quoll and the tiger quoll, both renowned for how endangered they are on the mainland. Tasmanian devils are another marvel that roamed the forests and paddocks down there, but sadly the first few I saw had been hit by cars.

In Tasmania, the human population is much smaller compared to the rest of Australia, meaning that animals are right up close to many busy roads. Possums and wallabies are hit the most, followed by the scavengers that feed on them – quolls, Tasmanian devils and birds of prey.

Once I read about the number of animals killed by cars alone in Tasmania, the hope I had harboured that Tasmanian wildlife was better protected was crushed pretty quickly.

In summertime, the reality of this was brutal. On my way to suss the surf or drive a few kilometres to a friend's house, I'd find myself pulling over to check ten or more dead animals that had been hit the night before. Some looked perfect, like they were just sleeping; others were like something out of a horror movie. As always, I took a deep breath, pushed my emotions and the sheer horror aside, and checked the animals, making sure to examine them for a joey-filled pouch. More often than not, the female wallabies, wombats, and possums did have joeys – but a lot of the time, the joeys had passed away, or, in worse cases, had been thrown out of the pouch on impact and run over.

The deaths were sad enough, but it was that people had just kept driving and clearly made no effort to move the animals off the road that made me so angry and upset. As much as I would like to say it's due to fear and a lack of education, I'm convinced a systemic lack of empathy and disregard for wildlife plays a role, too. Additionally, hunting, and shooting for fun under property protection permits, is very common in Tasmania – the rural areas especially. You can imagine that if someone with that mindset were to hit an animal, there's little chance they're going to go out of their way to help it.

I think that's what bothered me the most: the dissociation from wildlife was unlike what I'd experienced on mainland Australia. Sure, in some parts of Tasmania, like Hobart, there was a strong wildlife rescue presence – but up on the north-east coast, there was a huge desensitisation to hitting animals and thinking it was an issue.

Though this isn't isolated to Tasmania, it's just more obvious there due to the ratio of wild to populated areas. It was like it had become normal to people, not only because of the number of animals but also because most were tiny. It wasn't like in South Australia, where if you hit a full-size kangaroo or wombat, you would likely spin, crash or steer off the side of the road. If you hit a Tasmanian devil, you didn't risk dinging your bullbar, let alone writing off your car.

I will never forget one morning in particular. I was driving to the surf, and ahead of me was a straight road about one to two kilometres long. You could see the whole way very easily, and ahead of me on the other side of the road I could see a wallaby standing there. It was early in the morning, first light – a peak time for wildlife activity, so I was always on the lookout and driving cautiously at this time of the day.

Coming in the opposite direction was a white tray-back ute. Even though the wallaby was about 200 metres from the front of the car and directly in the way, even though I had slowed down and was flashing my lights at him, he wasn't slowing down at all. I watched as he hit the wallaby square on, going about 100 kilometres an hour. The wallaby didn't stand a chance – it was flung off the road and into the bushes. My whole body filled with rage. There was absolutely no way that the driver hadn't seen that wallaby standing there.

The car pulled over a few hundred metres up, as if to act like it had been an accident and he hadn't seen the wallaby … despite it being in clear sight and me flashing my lights. I knew that if I hadn't been there, imposing a need for him to take responsibility, he would have kept driving.

He came over to me and said, 'Where is it, do you need me to knock it on the head?'

'I don't know,' I said, disgusted. 'It'll be in a very bad way. We have to find it.'

'Nah,' he said. 'All good, it'll be sweet then.' And then he went back to his car and drove off.

I had literally watched this animal hit the bitumen in three different spots at 100 kilometres an hour. If it hadn't died on impact, it would be suffering immensely. Vibrating in anger, I walked through the thick scrub nearby, trying to listen for scuffling or any other noises, but I couldn't hear anything. There was dense scrub everywhere, and my chance of finding the wallaby was next to none. It had been conscious enough to make it somewhere far away before lying down, and I couldn't help it.

I went back to my car, feeling incredibly let down by humanity. I grew up with the moral to 'do for others as you wish would be done for you', and that extended to all living creatures. It was yet another blow to my perception that the world was becoming a better place, but I decided to use it to fuel my efforts, to keep working hard. We needed to do more.

Luckily, I was about to run into another little joey that would help restore my faith in Australia, and give me hope for conservation in Tasmania.

CHAPTER NINE

Saving Fern

I alone cannot change the world, but I can cast a stone across the waters to create many ripples.

Mother Teresa

The night I met Fern, we were at the wedding of some good friends of ours. It was held on a 40-acre property on the river, just up the road from our house, and the area was teeming with wildlife. Everyone was well into the booze and having a great time. I was coming back from the toilet when Mali, a good friend of mine, came looking for me. She was staying with her mum in their camper trailer on the side of the property among the trees; I followed Mali back there. Lila, Mali's mum, was standing there holding a beanie in her arms.

'We found a joey,' Lila explained. Mali had heard the clicking sound that baby wallabies or roos make when they've lost their mum or are stressed. Mali and Lila had walked over and scooped the little joey into a beanie, and didn't know what to do next.

Even though it was a wedding, I was sober. I'm pretty bad at drinking – I know my limit is about two drinks until I'm ready for bed – so I hadn't had a sip of alcohol yet.

'Let's take her home to my house,' I said. The party was loud, and we couldn't really see the joey properly in the camper trailer's light. 'I can check her out and we can make a plan.'

Back home, I did an initial check of the joey. Mali and I got her out of her beanie, laid her on the bed and had a look. She didn't have any noticeable physical injuries, but she was seriously weak and thin. Disturbingly, she was covered head to toe in thousands of maggots that were intertwined and stuck to her skin. It was disgusting. This meant that she had likely been in the pouch as her mum started to decompose and be consumed by parasites; the joey was being eaten alive.

Luckily, she had already made her way out of the pouch when we found her, so most of the maggots were dead.

I quickly ran a warm bath in our bathroom sink and put diluted Epsom salts, apple cider vinegar and coconut oil in the water. Epsom salts and apple cider vinegar are acidic, natural cleansers that wouldn't harm a joey's sensitive skin. Combined with the coconut oil, the bathwater would kill any of the maggots that didn't immediately drown. The oil also lubricated the joey's skin, making it easy for all the dead parasites to fall off. As I carefully bathed her, she immediately relaxed. It was like she knew she was in safe hands.

We got her all cleaned up, and then popped her into a clean pillowcase pouch followed by a thicker external pouch, both of which I had from my time with Bunji. I then popped her down my top. I had a very solid rescue kit at home for most wildlife, but I didn't have the right bottle teat for a joey this size, and I wanted a vet to check her for internal injuries.

I dropped Mali back at the wedding, and then drove to the closest after-hours vet to pick up the right bottle teat and get a quick X-ray. It turned out that the joey was completely fine, but just needed the usual: nutrition, a safe place to stay, and to get back up to a healthy weight. So I headed home, missed the rest of the wedding, and sat down to feed the little life that was now safe in my arms.

Mali and I named her Fern, after the forest she was found in.

The following months of Fern's journey were both fulfilling and heartwarming for me. After being faced with so many animals that had lost their lives, I had finally found one that I could help. During those weeks, I was put in touch with some amazing people around our area. It turned out there *were* some people out here who loved wildlife like I did – they just kept to themselves.

Fern spent the best part of the first few months hanging in a pouch off a sawhorse in our living room; it was full of natural light, and, with double-glazed windows, it was warm, quiet and had an incredible view facing east over the Scamander River. We were tucked away on seven acres of native bushland on a peaceful part of the north-east coast; it was a perfect hideaway for the animals that lived here, and a perfect view for Fern to watch as she progressed further and further into a curious furred joey.

Like Bunji at that age, Fern got three to four bottles a day and slept a lot at first. As she grew more curious, she slowly started doing small hops around the house. Our house was carpet, so it was a perfect learning ground for her to find her feet. She would go for small hops, have a little drink out of a tiny water dish, have a munch on some she-oak, then tumble back into her pouch.

Ohana and Rain were both very interested in the little addition to our household. As Ohana had grown up with Bunji, she knew immediately what Fern was, and would not leave her side. Ohana actually slept and laid under the pouch where Fern was hanging. Fern would hop up to Ohana and lie down right in front of her chest, almost nestling into her fluffy fur, and Ohana wouldn't move an inch. And, much like with Bunji, Ohana was in guardian mode. We put Fern into one of our free bedrooms at night-time to sleep in her hanging pouch, so that she was away from noises such as the TV. There were a few times when Fern had messed up her pouch and gotten out, then started calling for help while we were asleep. Ohana would go to Fern's door and start softly whimpering, and then come and get me. She was always right that Fern needed help.

Rain, meanwhile, had a much more timid nature. As she saw Ohana as an older sister and the boss, she hung back and observed. She loved Fern, though; they liked to boop each other on the nose, and Rain would often hang out nearby while Fern ate or had a bottle from us. Chippa was incredible with Fern too; he was generally great with animal care, and picked things up quickly as he went along. We took turns feeding and toileting her, doing our best to keep her healthy and strong.

As Fern grew more curious, I would spend time with her outside on our lawn, getting her used to the smells, sounds, trees and birds, and also letting her have a little dig or nibble on the dirt; it's important for their gut bacteria to develop, which they would normally get through their mother's milk. As I lay outside, watching her, there were so many times when I thought of Bunji. They had many similar mannerisms, like how they drank out of a bowl for the first time or the tiny noises they made as they hopped. Naturally, Fern and I bonded – but it was different, because I knew that she would eventually have a life somewhere wild. I tried to keep a bit of a barrier up with Fern, knowing that I only had her for a few months.

The difference between raising wallabies or kangaroos for release in Tasmania versus on the mainland is that in Tasmania, there are no native dog-like predators anymore. Tasmania did once have such an animal over a hundred years ago: the thylacine, or Tasmanian tiger, which was bounty hunted to extinction because it was falsely blamed for killing young livestock. In mainland Australia, though, the dingo is very much alive and well. Although Fern was unlikely to encounter a natural dog-like predator in the Tasmanian wilds, kangaroos' natural instinct as they get closer and closer to adulthood is to be wary of most larger animals – including humans, their greatest threat of all. I planned to preserve that instinct in Fern as much as possible.

I wanted to quickly partner Fern up with another wallaby; when it was time for her to go outside into a soft release area and then a larger area after that – maybe even the wild full-time – she would have someone to support her, which is essential for the health of wallabies and roos. I for sure had more experience as a wildlife carer, but I also knew first-hand that the longer you cared for the animal, the harder it was for both of you when you had to part ways.

I started searching for contacts who might be able to help. I was optimistic, but cautious; I didn't have an extensive network in Tasmania like I did on the mainland, and like in any profession or hobby, there are people in the wildlife carer community who make life hard for others. Instead of being inclusive and wanting to help each other, people can be very territorial and competitive. It doesn't make any sense to me – we all have the same goal! Plus, this sort of behaviour can get in the way of that goal.

Many of the best wildlife carers become carers by learning from established people in the community, which I always thought was powerful; the more people caring about these animals, the better. It wasn't always about having a qualification, but more about love, dedication and willingness to learn.

The wildlife carers in our area were few and far between, and, as I expected, quite reserved and off the grid. I loved this because it meant they were the real deal. The wildlife carers I've met who just do their thing and keep to themselves are some of the most passionate, dedicated people on the planet, and thankfully it was no different in Tasmania.

I ended up getting in touch with a lady called Sharlene. We first chatted on the phone about life, our love for animals and our mutual disinterest in getting involved in the politics of wildlife care. I knew pretty quickly that she was like me, and that we were going to get along. I had originally contacted her in the hope that she might have a buddy that our little Fern could partner up with, but I got lucky: Sharlene thought she might be able to take Fern on long-term.

Sharlene lived on 30 acres deep within the forest, off a winding road kilometres from any town. Her house was at the end of many dirt roads and tracks, full of turns you could only navigate with her directions. After carefully following her instructions, I came to an opening in the forest. As I pulled up in my Landcruiser, forester kangaroos stared at me, a wombat stopped munching on the green grass and a sheep started baaing. I loved this place already. I'd never seen anywhere so perfect for rescuing wildlife. It was a safe haven.

In South Australia, it's illegal to rerelease rescue animals, for good reason – but Tasmania has different laws fitting its environment. Sharlene's home, hidden so far into her rescue animals' native habitat, meant that rerelease was not only an option, but a goal.

Sharlene had long blonde hair, a huge smile and a soul made from pure kindness. She was middle-aged and was always walking around with one or two joeys tucked into a pouch in her arms. She told me about her journey of wildlife care in Tasmania; she had experience raising almost every species that roamed the island. Possums, Tasmanian devils, quolls, birds of prey, wallabies, dogs, cats – the list goes on. The sheep that had baaed as I came in had been abandoned during the winter lambing months, and she had a cat that she had found as a tiny stray kitten. Her empathy for animals was the same as mine: she didn't criticise or pick and choose based on species. From there, our friendship bloomed.

Sharlene's property was perfect for all kinds of wildlife on their rehab journeys. There were enclosures and soft release pens for wombats, possums, roos and wallabies. The cat had his own special cat run and catio, so that he had space outside but wasn't free-roaming in the forest. He was the gentlest cat I'd ever met, just lazing in front of the fire next to a joey. I loved it up there.

Sharlene had another Bennett's wallaby that was around the same age as Fern, as well as a pademelon, and some forester joeys. She was more than happy to take Fern and buddy her up with one of the joeys she already had. And, because Fern was so young, her transition to this new home was quite easy. It was still a transition, but because she was still in the pouch on many bottles a day, it was a great time to get her into a home that she could eventually treat as a base while having the freedom to go in and out of the forest. I was thrilled and relieved to have met such an incredible person, and also to have such a solid plan for Fern so early.

Fern settled in nicely to life in her new forest home. I visited often, not only to check in and give Fern lots of little kisses but also to hang out with all the other incredible animals, which included a number of wombats that Sharlene had hand-raised and released. The wombats would go about their day in the forest and then, most afternoons, come back to hang out in the clearing at Sharlene's house. It was a true safe haven for all the animals that were lucky enough to be rescued and released on this property.

I was able to donate some funds from Balu Blue to help cover the costs of food and vet bills for the animals, which Sharlene always prioritised over her own needs. I wished I could help more, but I was grateful to be able to help at all – and also just for meeting Sharlene and seeing what she does silently for so many animals.

CHAPTER TEN

Bringing Balu Blue to the public

I believe animals should be respected as citizens of the earth. They should have the right to their own freedom, their own families, their own life.

John Feldmann

After spending a year or so in Tasmania, Chippa and I decided to move back to Western Australia. Being back on the mainland held more opportunities for the both of us, and we knew we would regularly visit Tasmania. We ended up finding a property with several acres – perfect for our lifestyle and beautiful dogs. We were ready to start the next stage in our life together, both personally and professionally. Balu Blue was going well, but I never felt like it was enough. I wanted to do even more.

I had been in contact with so many amazing wildlife organisations and carers in my time travelling around Australia, and while the passion and drive seemed consistent, the level of knowledge and connections that people had varied wildly. For quite some time, I had sensed a big gap between wildlife carers, and veterinarians. The gap was even bigger between these people and the everyday person who wants to help an animal when the situation arises. For example, if you hit an animal while driving, assisting the animal is a simple process – but very few people stop to help, partly because they just don't know what to do. Despite how much it upsets me to see these animals on the road, I have come across hurdles in my own journey that made me realise how difficult it could seem to someone who has no experience to get an animal help. What do they do? Who do they call if there's no vet nearby?

The issue of animals in need stems far deeper than just kangaroos on our roads, of course. There's a distinct lack of help for marine life – for example, I was so sad to find out that in Tasmania, if you find a seal or sea lion that had fallen victim to fishing lines or a boat strike, there are no official government organisations you can reach out to. Parks departments simply don't have the facilities, and so the seals would simply be put down despite there sometimes being a strong chance for survival and high quality of life with the right treatment. Being able to rehabilitate marine life was, and still is, very high on the list for Balu Blue. However, regulations around marine life are, in general more complex than those for land wildlife, so any campaigns from Balu Blue would have to come further down the line. I had to work with what I could in the meantime.

When I launched Balu Blue, one of the first things we put together was a rescue guide that people could print out and keep in their car; it was intended as a resource to use if you hit a kangaroo (or found one that someone else had hit), including what to do if there is an orphaned joey. It was a priority for us because it's the most common wildlife accident in Australia, and knowing how easy it is to just stop and check, I wanted to give people the tools and confidence to do it themselves. It was a simple, step-by-step guide, but people still had to print it out. That step was a roadblock for a lot of people; not many people have access to a printer at home, or the money and time to go and get it printed elsewhere. Plus, what if they didn't have the guide nearby during the one time they needed it? It seemed like a no-brainer to convert the guide to an app and greatly expand its contents. Everyone uses their phones for everything these days, and converting it into an app meant we could regularly update it and integrate it with a phone's camera and call functions. Not only would it give people the knowledge to help the animal, but it could also tell people who to contact for help! This then sparked the idea of marking wildlife hotspots, which could help gather crucial data such as where wildlife were regularly crossing roads or falling victim to entanglement, boat strikes and more. This app had the potential to make a huge impact if it was built with the ability to allow us to continue adding to it, and if it was fun, educational and easily accessible. It needed to be something people could lean on when they found an animal in need.

Coming from a marine science and animal rescue background, though, the world of app development and everything that comes with it wasn't exactly my forte. It was very new ground for me. I chatted to a few close friends about the idea to gauge the process: which app developers were reliable? How long would it take? How much would it cost, both upfront and long-term? I was grateful to have a friend offer to manage the project for me, and they put me in contact with some developers in America and India who cared about the cause and would be able to help.

Fast forward two years, and the amount of time I had put into this project was astonishing. Developing an app was something I never imagined I would do. I wasn't aware of the continuous hurdles and costs that you come across while building an app. In the beginning, things were really exciting and progressed quickly, but as the project came to an end, I found I had poured my heart and soul (and Balu Blue's funds!) into the idea and had an app that was nowhere near the scale of what I had imagined.

It had cost us close to $100,000 due to the unexpected development challenges surrounding the use of Google Maps, which we needed for marking hotspots, and we were definitely not getting our money's worth. We desperately needed a finished product so that we could go to sponsors and get all of that money back; we were such a small volunteer team, and that money had been saved for a large project as amazing as this one. It couldn't go to waste. I spent countless hours on it. I collated all of the rescue guides with the assistance of different wildlife carers and advisors along the way, trying to make the information accurate and informative while also keeping it simple.

I also had to gather as many wildlife contacts as I could around the country, to make the app sufficient to launch – a mammoth job, one so large that a friend assisted me. Many wildlife carers are private carers; you can't just put their address in a public app. We needed to use the coordinates of their nearest town so they would show up in the app if someone was in that area and in need of their services. There were hundreds of carers and that was before we checked off the more well-known carers and organisations. We also needed to coordinate with designers and artists to help make the app look inviting and eye-catching. In among all this information gathering and liaising, there was so many conversations back and forth with the developers, who weren't able to met our app's needs. This was frustrating, and also extremely expensive – we were on a monthly building retainer, which was in US dollars. By the time we realised we were exceeding our budget without meeting our vision for the app, we had come too far to pull out and find someone else.

While we ended up with a working app, it wasn't how I imagined it. I wanted people to be excited to use the app – to be excited to help all animals. I wanted it to be a fun educational activity for kids beyond its use as an emergency tool. I wanted it to be an app for all animal rescues, and all marine life – not just land-based wildlife. I wanted it to connect carers, vets, animal rescues and more all around Australia. I wanted this app to change things, to change lives. So while I was exhausted, I wasn't ready to give up. In early 2023, I dug a little deeper in my contacts and got put in touch with two good friends.

We re-evaluated the whole project and moved to a new developer ... and they were shocked at how bad the original build was. It made my heart sink, but you can only work with what you have at the time; I took it on the chin and moved forward. We would make the app better than ever, and aim to bring it to Australian users in 2024 – bigger, better, bolder and ready to save more animals. At the time of writing, the app is still in development as we secure further funding. Keep an eye out for an app called 'Arky' – it just might just help you save lives.

We're also working on new projects that educate and inspire people, and continue to fight for animals, land and sea. We've been doing our best to grow Balu Blue as a leading organisation in marine animal conservation and public education, focusing on kindness to, and empathy for, our wildlife. We've had some major wins: collaborating with other like-minded groups, raising awareness for wildlife through community-focused initiatives, and pushing for change on a political level (such as our shark net campaign in New South Wales and Queensland, and our campaign to ban the cruel treatment of bats in Queensland). There's so much more to do, and the work is never done – but it's a start.

CHAPTER ELEVEN

A happy ending and a bright future

The best time to plant a tree was twenty years ago. The second best time is now.

Anon

As I look back on this journey and relive these moments, the huge influence my experience with Bunji had on my path up until this point is undeniable. Bunji came into my life at the start of what felt like a turning point for me and my career; I learnt sacrifice, strength, courage and trust, on top of endless teachings about not only kangaroos, but also the many other species out in the wild facing the same day-to-day threats. Bunji taught me that love trumps all doubt; the attachment animals have to those they see as their loved ones and family – whether they're differing species or not – is not at all different to us humans and our children. Whenever I visit Bunji and watch her run across the paddock to me, an act of affection she performs for no one else, I can't stop myself from crying tears of pure happiness and love. The hugs she gives are the highlight of my year. Part of me will always wish I lived around the corner, but if I did, she might never have formed a lifelong friendship with George, her fellow Euro kangaroo. She might never have grown into the resilient, independent, wonderful being she is. My visits always mean I'm going back to what is best for her, and that gives me great joy and pride.

Luckily, it never feels like she's far away. There is a big Euro roo who lives on our street here on the Ningaloo, and each day I see him, I just sit and watch and adore him from afar. We've also added another small family member to our crew: Manta, a stray kitten found on our local streets and handed in to the vet. Ohana is already teaching Manta her ways, and Rain plays with Manta like the adopted siblings they are. Manta even loves swimming at the beach with Ohana and Rain – a sight that always reminds me of the day Bunji first went swimming with Ohana. It fills my heart up again knowing that love, trust and a safe home always paves the path to a happy rescue story.

Bunji's story is indeed just that: a happy rescue story. Her journey drove my passions and dedication to speaking up for animals, and pushed me out of my comfort zone. I still stop to check the pouches of roos that have been hit on the road, despite the regular heartache and anger it results in. I know with confidence now that if I find a surviving joey, so many wonderful people will make the effort alongside me to help. Bunji's story has helped me reach so many people and give them that same gift of confidence and sense of support; I'll never stop sharing her story with everyone I meet as I continue along my path in conservation. Thanks to her I have seen many beautiful things and saved many beautiful animals. As Charles Darwin once said, 'The love for all living creatures is the most noble attribute of man.' Because of Bunji, decades from now I will be able to look back and know that by telling our story, I was doing something tangible – something that contributed towards a better future.

Author's note

As you might have figured out by now, one of my greatest goals is to inspire people to extend their kindness and compassion to all species. I hope reading *Saving Bunji* has educated you a little on the importance of wildlife, and maybe inspired you to do more in your own life to support our beautiful animal friends.

The natural world faces immense pressure from climate change and many other challenges that are yet to be overcome. Of course, addressing systemic issues will be beyond many readers' capabilities. Faced with such difficult obstacles, we must remain positive and focus on what we can do rather than what we can't do.

This is why I think it is so important to step into action when you see an animal suffering. You might choose to drive past an animal in need of help because you assume someone else will do it, or has done it – but if you're thinking that, it's likely the vast majority of other passers-by are thinking that too. This goes for when you are in the ocean as well, such as if you find an animal entangled, stuck or stranded. The likelihood of someone else stopping is very, very low. If you were to be in the same scenario, how would you like to be treated?

Us humans are an intelligent species, and prove time and time again that we are able to make huge changes when we work together. I've always prided myself on my ability to have open dialogue with people from industries I disagree with – not to make them feel guilty about the place they work or their lifestyle, but to lead by example and educate them on other options that benefit everyone living on this planet.

With this in mind, I've added a 'further reading' section to provide you with further information on some of the more divisive topics I've touched on in this book. I encourage you to read with an open mind, and maybe engage a little more with how you live your life.

Imagine how the world could be if we were all connected to nature once again, and allowed ourselves to see animals as they are: unique, loving individuals with a rich internal life all of their own.

I think our world would be a much kinder place. Don't you?

Brinkley Davies

Balu Blue Foundation
www.balubluefoundation.org
@balubluefoundation on Instagram and Facebook

The benefits of veganism and sustainable living

While I grew up around many families who only caught the fish they needed and grew their own vegetables, many people are completely disconnected from the production of their food. It's hard to comprehend the sheer damage that globally growing 60 billion farm animals for human consumption can cause, from their poor quality of life to the sheer volume of land and feed required. The devastating fact is that our oceans are screaming for help, with over 4.6 million commercial fishing vessels operating worldwide, resulting in an appalling amount of bycatch, loss of ecological balance, and pollution. It would be enough to make anyone want to take fish off their plates – but most people just don't realise how big a problem it is. If everyone in the world swapped to a plant-based diet, we would reduce global agricultural land use from 4 to 1 billion hectares. Think of everything we could do with that extra land to improve the planet! Not to mention, it would cut global greenhouse emissions in half.

If you are unsure where to start your plant-based journey, I recommend hopping online and looking through the recipes uploaded by the well-known chefs who live a delicious vegan lifestyle, such as Shannon Martinez. If swapping to a plant-based diet isn't an option for you yet, I encourage you to try to take small steps. Trying to cut back your animal-based consumption and be more aware of where you're getting your food from is a huge part. Keep in mind that animals, despite being labelled as 'free range' or 'grass fed' may still be raised to feel like family, only to end up on the dinner table. For your own wellbeing, I urge you to consider the question: if this harm isn't necessary, then why partake in it?

Our wardrobes also often inadvertently support industries we would rather avoid supporting. Cheap clothing often means cheap materials, cheap labour and a cheap shot at the planet. When possible, fill your wardrobe with things that last and make use of op shops to purchase preloved clothing. Additionally, try alternative products; rather than leather, try recycled synthetics, biodegradable cork, and fruit agricultural waste such as Piñatex (made from pineapples!). Or, rather than wool (its removal can be inherently harmful to many sheep breeds, and the industry damages the land and harms wildlife), try Tencel or bamboo lyocell, which has similar thermoregulating properties to wool, is made in a closed-loop system, and is sustainably sourced.

- If the world adopted a plant-based diet we would reduce global agricultural land use from 4 to 1 billion hectares

  (Hannah Ritchie. *Our World in Data*, March 2021)

  www.ourworldindata.org/land-use-diets

- The state of world fisheries and aquaculture

  (Food and Agriculture Organization of the United Nations, 2016)

  www.fao.org/3/i5555e/i5555e.pdf

- Global greenhouse gas emissions from animal-based foods are twice those of plant-based foods

  (X. Xu et al. *Food and Agriculture Organisation of the United Nations*, 2021)

  www.fao.org/publications/card/en/c/CB7033EN

- Bycatch and its impacts

  (*International Whaling Commission*, 2023)

  www.iwc.int/bycatch

- Alternatives to leather, and other animal products

  (*Collective Fashion Justice*, 2023)

  www.collectivefashionjustice.org/leather-alternatives

- Six things the fishing industry doesn't want you to know

  (*Animals Australia,* 2023)

  www.animalsaustralia.org/our-work/marine-animals/about-the-fishing-industry

- An incredible fish friendship

  (*Animals Australia,* 2022)

  www.animalsaustralia.org/our-work/marine-animals/puffer-fish-friends

- A transition away from industrialised fishing and farming

  (*Defend the Wild*, 2023)

  https://www.defendthewild.org/agricultural-transition

- You didn't know, did you? Help farmed animals

  (*Animals* Australia, 2023)

  https://animalsaustralia.org/our-work/farmed-animals/you-didnt-know-did-you

Roadkill statistics

Driving at night can be stressful enough without having to worry about animals crossing the road. As I've made clear in *Saving Bunji*, people accidentally (or even deliberately!) hitting animals and then leaving them to die is a huge problem. Kangaroos alone make up 90 per cent of animal crashes in New South Wales, with 10 million animals being hit each year in Australia – that's a lot of little Bunjis at risk out there. There are ways you can minimise the risk of hitting an animal, such as driving slowly, keeping alert and avoiding high crossing times such as dawn and dusk. If you do find yourself in a situation where you can help an animal, do it. It's a huge step towards respect and coexistence. Our app Arky will provide key resources to assist in not only rescue situations, but marking roadkill or crossing areas for data collection and further protection of these areas. Visit the resources here for more information.

- Kangaroos account for 90 per cent of crashes involving animals in NSW, so what do you do if you hit a roo?

  (Ann Carter, Jen Browning. *ABC News*, June 2019)

  www.abc.net.au/news/2019–06–22/you-have-hit-a-roo-so-what-do-you-do-next/11235596

- Australia's 'road kill' map: The 76-year old making a road kill map of Australia

  (Eloise Gibson. *BBC Earth*, November 2019)

  www.bbcearth.com/news/australias-road-kill-map

- 10 million+ animals are hit on our roads each year. Here's how you can help them (and steer clear of them) these holidays

  (Marissa Parrott. *The Conversation*, December 2020)

  www.theconversation.com/10-million-animals-are-hit-on-our-roads-each-year-heres-how-you-can-help-them-and-steer-clear-of-them-these-holidays-149733

Australian agriculture and the kangaroo

Kangaroos are arguably the most iconic and globally recognised native Australian animal, and have lived here for 20 million years, playing a vital role in our ecosystems and regeneration of native plants. Even now, their feeding habits reduce fuel loads that can cause wildfire in forests and grasslands. Despite this, the killing of kangaroos for pet food or leather is justified by an inaccurate and morally repugnant 'pest species' status in the agricultural world.

Kangaroo leather has long been utilised by the sporting industry, particularly for making football boots, and their flesh is used widely in the pet food industry, as well as being sold for human consumption. Both kangaroo meat and leather are incorrectly promoted as more ethical or sustainable products for consumers to choose.

As you might imagine, this industry is full of unseen cruelty; non-fatal shots are an inherent part of the industry, prolonging suffering and pain. There is also no law to protect mother kangaroos still nurturing dependant joeys from being shot and killed. Depending on the age and the size of the surviving joey, the hunter is legally allowed to kill an orphan joey by 'cervical dislocation' (aka decapitation), a heavy blow to the head with rocks or metal poles, or a gunshot to the head/chest. It's estimated that 440,000 joeys are legally killed or left to starve each year by shooters. It's a staggering number, and this industry continues despite multiple leather alternatives. At least commercial shooters can lose their license if they make regular non-fatal shots; this doesn't apply to non-commercial shooters, such as farmers, so you can only imagine the results.

- What is the difference between non-commercial and commercial kangaroo shooting?
    (*RSPCA*, 2020)
    kb.rspca.org.au/knowledge-base/what-is-the-difference-between-non-commercial-and-commercial-kangaroo-shooting

- Issues in the kangaroo skin leather supply chain
    (*Collective Fashion Justice*, 2023)
    www.collectivefashionjustice.org/kangaroo-leather

- Welfare issues in the kangaroo product industry
    (*International Kangaroo Protection Alliance*, 2023)
    www.kangarooprotection.org/category/welfare

- Make a powerful change for kangaroos and their joeys

    (*Animals* Australia, 2022)

    www.animalsaustralia.org/our-work/
    wildlife/protect-kangaroos-and-joeys

- Save them or kill them: Australians divided on kangaroos

    (*The Sydney Morning Herald, 2015*)

    www.smh.com.au/environment/
    conservation/save-them-or-kill-them-
    australians-divided-on-kangaroos-20150126

- Australia has been home to hopping kangaroos for 20 million years

    (*New Scientist, 2019*)

    https://www.newscientist.com/
    article/2192710-australia-has-been-home-
    to-hopping-kangaroos-for-20-million-years

1080 baits and the harm of toxic poisons

I once wanted to be a ranger for national parks here in Australia, until I realised that as a park ranger, you have to be a part of the 1080 baiting program for species (invasive or otherwise) that are either too smart to take them, or are in the area at all. Even disregarding the ethics of bait programs, their ineffectiveness means many baits are left littered around the countryside for non-targeted species – like my Balu – to consume. These baits, which are 'systematically' distributed by being chucked off a moving vehicle, or out of a plane, cause a slow and immensely painful death, involving hours of internal bleeding and seizures. Studies show that the industry perception of these baits being humane is incorrect, but the government has yet to act on these findings. I urge you to educate yourself on these baits, poisons that harm the entire ecosystem, such as mouse or ant poison, and other outdated lethal measures which are harming our wildlife every day, and join the fight against them. This attitude towards introduced species needs to change; nature has the ability to balance itself if we let it, rather than try to 'play god'. We can't pick and choose which animals we think deserve special treatment and which don't. We must learn to coexist with animals, and not simply take or push blame onto them.

- Is sodium fluoroacetate (1080) a humane poison?

  (Miranda Sherley. Universities Federation for Animal Welfare, 2007)

  www.researchgate.net/publication/228620466_Is_sodium_fluoroacetate_1080_a_humane_poison

- The dog fence: what future for this iconic, but contentious barrier?

  (Justine Philip. *Australian Geographic*)

  www.australiangeographic.com.au/topics/science-environment/2022/05/the-dog-fence-3

- Take action against 1080 poison

  (*Ban 1080*, 2023)

  https://www.ban1080.org.au/take-action

- *The New Wild: Why Invasive Species Will Be Nature's Salvation*

  (Fred Pearce, Icon Books, 2016)

- Native animals, poisoned, trapped, shot

  (*Animals Australia*, 2023)

  https://animalsaustralia.org/our-work/wildlife/take-action-for-dingoes

Giving the land back to the traditional owners

I feel it would be remiss to talk about ways we can help heal Australia without touching on one of the biggest sources of pain for Australia full-stop, which also in turn affects our local land and wildlife.

The traditional owners lived sustainably in Australia for more than 65,000 years before European colonisation, largely relying on cultivation of native fruits and vegetables and complemented by traditional hunting practices. Their ability to sustain and manage areas such as national parks, which were once rightfully theirs, should be a priority, especially when we consider the lasting ecological damage caused by colonisers ill equipped to manage the Australian landscape.

Handing back land rights to the traditional owners and working together would see a rewilding of the landscape, vastly improving the ecosystem. If you care about renewing the environment, it's worth considering the role that the Land Back movement should play in that and supporting political change to enable it.

- Return the land
    (*Defend the Wild*, 2023)
    www.defendthewild.org/return-the-land.

- Indigenous land management in Australia: a summary of the extent, barriers and success factors
    (Ro Hill et al. CSIRO, 2013)
    www.agriculture.gov.au/sites/default/files/sitecollectiondocuments/natural-resources/landcare/submissions/ilm-factsheet.pdf

- We just Black matter: Australia's indifference to Aboriginal lives and land
    (Chelsea Watego. *The Conversation*, October 2017)
    www.theconversation.com/we-just-black-matter-australias-indifference-to-aboriginal-lives-and-land-85168

- Australians Together Learning Framework
    (*Australians Together*, 2023)
    www.australianstogether.org.au/discover-and-learn

- Australia's moral legitimacy depends on recognising Indigenous sovereignty
    (Marcia Langton. *ABC News*, July 2019)
    www.abc.net.au/religion/marcia-langton-australia-moral-legitimacy-and-indigenous-sovere/11287908

Acknowledgements

There are so many people to acknowledge in this journey, so I will do my best.

Firstly, the traditional owners of all the lands I get to live and love on – of lands and seas I constantly speak up for and always will.

My parents, Tracey, and Brett, who have individually taught me so much, and have huge hearts for not just nature, but all living things. To my brother Jedd, for challenging me my whole childhood, teaching me to keep up with the boys, and always being there as one of my closest people. Chippa, for being by my side during the journey, making me laugh and making me happy every day, and supporting me not only during love, life and passion, but also through the heartache that comes with saving animals. To Linda and Bronte, for being two of the most selfless people I have ever met and dedicating your life to starting Two Songs; for giving animals, including Bunji, a loving home. To Sharlene, who also dedicates her life to rescuing animals, and taking on Fern. To all my closest friends, who have changed their lives and listened to my stories long before I wrote this book, who now share those passions with their families. My animals, Ohana, Rain and Manta, who show me unconditional love and happiness, and make me feel fulfilled every day. To everyone who has helped or assisted in

not only Bunji's journey, but any of our goals and projects with Balu Blue Foundation, and who have believed in my vision and passion for greater protection of animals.

Finally, to each and every person who has ever helped an animal in need, spoken up for something that needs to change, or believes that together we have the power to change the world to see a kinder future. We need you. Kindness and love – they rule the world. To march forward with a positive attitude despite the grief in the world, to march forward with grace when stones are thrown our way, and to be fearlessly speaking up for what is right, despite the backlash – these are the people I acknowledge. You are all leaders, and you hold the future in your hands.